CHRIST&
NARCISSUS

CHRIST&
NARCISSUS

Prayer
in a
Self-Centered
World

Warren McWilliams

HERALD PRESS
Scottdale, Pennsylvania
Waterloo, Ontario

Library of Congress Cataloging-in-Publication Data
McWilliams, Warren, 1946-
   Christ and Narcissus : prayer in a self-centered world / Warren McWilliams.
      p. cm.
   Includes bibliographical references.
   ISBN 0-8361-3569-5 (alk. paper)
   1. Prayer. 2. Lord's prayer. 3. Narcissism. I. Title.
BV210.2.M39 1992
248.3'2—dc20
                                        91-36400
                                        CIP

The paper used in this publication is recycled and meets the minimum requirements of American National Standard for Information Sciences—Permanence of Paper for Printed Library Materials, ANSI Z39.48-1984.

Unless otherwise marked, Scripture quotations are from the *Holy Bible: New International Version*. Copyright © 1973, 1978, 1984 International Bible Society. Used by permission of Zondervan Bible Publishers.

Scripture quotations marked RSV are from the Revised Standard Version of the Bible, copyright 1946, 1952, 1971 by the Division of Christian Education of the National Council of the Churches of Christ in the USA. Used by permission.

Scripture quotation marked Phillips is From *The New Testament in Modern English*, Revised Edition, © J. B. Phillips 1958, 1960, 1972. By permission of Macmillan Publishing Co., Inc., and William Collins Sons & Co., Ltd.

Grateful acknowledgment is made for permission to adapt ideas from "Christ or Narcissus? Ministry in a Self-Centered Culture," by Warren McWilliams, *Search*, Fall 1988 © Copyright 1988 the Sunday School Board of the Southern Baptist Convention. All rights reserved. Used by permission.

CHRIST AND NARCISSUS
Copyright © 1992 by Herald Press, Scottdale, Pa. 15683
   Published simultaneously in Canada by Herald Press,
   Waterloo, Ont. N2L 6H7. All rights reserved.
Library of Congress Catalog Number: 91-36400
International Standard Book Number: 0-8361-3569-5
Printed in the United States of America
Cover and book design by Gwen Stamm

1 2 3 4 5 6 7 8 9 10 97 96 95 94 93 92

Dedicated to the faculty
of the Joe L. Ingram School of Christian Service
Oklahoma Baptist University

Contents

Preface

On a trip to Stratford-upon-Avon in England, I noticed a friend looking for a small statue of Shakespeare in a gift shop. When I asked why he wanted such a souvenir, he replied that he had a large collection of statues of "gods." Some of these gods were from the world's religions, but others were statues of famous people revered or idolized by people today. He did not worship any of these gods, but they represented the human tendency to turn something or someone into a god.

A thesis of this book is that a large number of contemporary Americans have made Narcissus, a figure in Greek mythology, their god. Narcissus loved himself so much that he gazed endlessly at his reflection in a pool of water. *Narcissism* has become a convenient label for excessive self-love and preoccupation with self. Although narcissism may characterize humanity throughout all its history, many analysts of culture have noted an intensification of narcissism in our recent history.

Can Christians love themselves without becoming narcissists? Can narcissists be changed from an egocentric lifestyle to a Christocentric lifestyle? In this study the relation of Christ and Narcissus will be the focus of concern. *Christ and Narcissus* is a case study within the larger discussion of Christ and culture. How does a Christian relate to the prevailing culture of his or her day? This book will explore narcissism as one of the dominant attitudes of our day, but a full study of Christ and culture could look at many other attitudes.

Popular culture will offer one source of illustration and illumination of contemporary narcissism and its permeation of our culture. Films, television, and comic strips reflect the conventional wisdom of our culture. Believers and nonbelievers alike are influenced by the concern for self-fulfillment and self-help.

Although we will look at many aspects of a Christian response to narcissism, a Christian view of prayer will be central. Distinctively Christian prayer provides a way for God to transform our character. The Lord's Prayer is an excellent summary of many of the central convictions of the Christian life, including both beliefs and behavior. How should a Christian pray when our culture encourages preoccupation with self? Can we pray for ourselves? We will explore these and other questions, using the Bible as primary source for determining a Christian view of prayer.

My work on this project was facilitated by several people. As usual, my wife, Patty, and my daughters Amy and Karen encouraged me. The members of University Baptist Church continue to share their worship and prayers with me. I have dedicated this book to my colleagues in the Joe L. Ingram School of Christian Service at Oklahoma Baptist University. No one could wish for a better community of faith and scholarship in which to serve.

Warren McWilliams
Auguie Henry Chair of Bible
Oklahoma Baptist University
Shawnee, Oklahoma

1

What Would We Gain by Praying?

The prayer preceding all prayers is "May it be the real I who speaks. May it be the real Thou that I speak to." [1] *C. S. Lewis*

Do you have a fundamental guiding principle for your life? In a comic strip one person says he knows many people today do not have high principles, but *he* does. He never deviates from that principle. When his friend asks what the principle is, the first person says, "Look out for number one."

Looking out for number one has been common in the last few decades as our culture has increasingly affirmed placing self-interest first. What should be the Christian's relationship to the prevailing culture? In his classic study, *Christ and Culture*, H. Richard Niebuhr described this issue as an "enduring problem" for Christians.[2] We can begin to see the specific shape of this issue by asking two questions: 1) What one value or belief should characterize Christians? 2) What one value or belief characterizes North American culture in the last part of the twentieth century?

Niebuhr did not attempt to isolate one dominant value for our century. He believed, however, that cultures tend to value what is good for human beings. Culture is generally *anthropocentric*, but it is not necessarily *narcissistic*.[3]

In this study three basic concerns will guide our reflection. First, we will explore narcissism as a prevailing value or belief of our culture. Named after the legendary Greek figure Narcissus, narcissism has become a popular label for attitudes such as self-love, self-actualization, and self-sufficiency. As a working definition, narcissism refers to an unhealthy preoccupation with self that distorts a person's relationship to God, other people, nature, and himself or herself. Second, we will examine the relationship between Christianity and narcissism. Narcissism is both a rival to Christianity and a view that affects Christians. Our study, then, is a case study in the "Christ and culture" discussion.

Third, we will suggest that Christian prayer provides one of the best ways of responding to narcissism. What we really value and believe is reflected in our prayers. Other aspects of Christian belief and behavior will be integral to our study, but essentially we will be developing a theology of prayer. As Emil Brunner suggested, "Prayer is the touchstone of faith, and the theology of prayer is the touchstone of all theology."[4] Although we will not attempt a comprehensive study of every theological aspect of prayer, we will highlight the relation of Christian prayer to narcissism. A clear understanding of Christian prayer clarifies the tension between Christ and Narcissus and helps us overcome the influence of narcissism. In other words, a theology of prayer is part of the diagnosis and the cure.

The tension between the Christian faith and narcissism can be illustrated by comparing two pray-ers, Joe and Jane, and their prayers.[5] Joe was a very prosperous, successful man who was also very immoral. Despite Joe's lack of moral integrity, he was extremely powerful, his children were successful in school, and his business was running at peak efficiency. Joe was not an atheist, yet he rarely thought about God and never saw the need for addressing God directly in prayer. In fact, Joe was certain his life could not be improved by bringing God into the picture. If he were to speak to God, his prayer would probably be: "Let me alone, God! I don't want you messing up my life. Anyway, what could I possibly gain by praying to you?" Joe had it all: money, power, career, popularity, and family. How could praying to God add to that?

The second pray-er, Jane, is a suburban homemaker, wife, and mother of four children. She does not see herself as particularly devout, although she and her family do attend church regularly. One night, after the children are asleep, she tells her husband that she realizes how fortunate they are to have such a happy family. Her situation is very similar to Joe's. She prays: "Dear God, thank you for everything. Amen." This time we catch a glimpse of some of the heavenly reaction. The angels are surprised that Jane did not make any requests. She did not ask for anything! Of course, at other times Jane did make requests, but this time she simply expressed gratitude.

To the theologically sensitive observer one significant difference between Joe and Jane is their attitude toward prayer. Both are successful by contemporary standards, but Joe sees no need to pray, and Jane spontaneously thanks God. At the risk of offering caricatures, the observer might label Joe as a narcissist and Jane as a Christian.

Joe's story seems more contemporary: he is the typical urban, secular person in the late twentieth century. Not an avowed atheist, he simply sees no need for God or prayer. His life is already complete without any conscious need for God, the transcendent, or institutional religion. Actually, Joe's story is told in the Bible. Successful, secular people have been around for a long, long time. Job, agonizing in the midst of his tragic circumstances, was troubled as well by the prosperity of people like Joe, people who bluntly asked about God: "What would we gain by praying to him?" (Job 21:15).

Jane's story may seem less realistic, more old-fashioned. Although it was based on a comic strip in the newspaper, it does reflect the experience of some Christians. They're not super-Christians or "saints" in the popular sense. People such as Jane do sometimes approach God with a shopping list, and gratitude might be only a minor part of their prayer life. Yet Jane's prayers are not dominated by Joe's "What's in it for me?" attitude.

In this chapter we will focus on several aspects of one basic question: What is prayer? In the next chapter we will turn to some related questions of utmost concern to a narcissist: Why pray? What motivates our prayer? What should be our agenda when we pray? Can we pray for ourselves without falling victim to narcissism?

What is prayer? Often when I teach theology, I ask my students to give their view of some doctrine in 25 words or less. How would you define prayer in 25 words or less? A common, simple definition of prayer is "talking with God."[6] Basically prayer is a conversation or dialogue with God. Theology is talking about God, but prayer is talking *with* God. Our study might be called a theology of prayer since we are trying to clarify the Christian understanding of prayer. We will primarily talk *about* God, but when we pray we are talking to or with God.

There are numerous dimensions or facets to prayer, but at the very least it involves us and God in a dialogue. The Lewis quotation that began the chapter reminds us that prayer ideally begins with an acknowledgment of the real God and of our real identity as human beings.

In examining the nature of prayer, we will address three issues. First, we will look at prayer as an action of the total person. Second, we will consider some inadequate views of prayer and the need for the proper audience, God. Third, we will explain why we will focus our study primarily on the Lord's Prayer or Model Prayer of Jesus.

Praying with the Spirit and the Mind

Who is the worst Christian you know? You may know several people, including yourself, who really struggle with putting their faith into practice, but here we mean true hypocrites. What they practice and what they preach are totally opposed (Matt. 23:3).

The worst Christian I know (whom I dare mention in print) is Frank Burns on the television series M*A*S*H. Besides Father Mulcahy, the chaplain, Frank was the most overtly pious character of the show. Frank was the character we loved to hate, however, because his piety was so superficial and shallow. Like many

of us, Frank put his religious convictions into a neat compart-
ment and isolated his piety from the rest of his life. He was a liar,
an adulterer, and a racist, but he acted like religion was important to him. In one episode Frank asked Margaret, "Whatever
happened to meat and potatoes Christianity?"

To me the answer is obvious: Frank Burns. Many people are
turned off by Christianity because of hypocritical Christians like
Frank Burns.

Because of people like Frank Burns we need to expand and re-
fine our definition of prayer. Prayer is *conversation with God by the
total person, whose entire life is oriented to the will of God.* The apostle
Paul never defined prayer in these words, but he reflected this
view in 1 Corinthians. Paul was deeply disturbed by the disunity
and immaturity in the Corinthian church. Part of the difficulty
was caused by a group that had special religious experiences and
promoted some spiritual gifts as the best.

As part of his response, Paul compared two types of prayer:
prayer with the *spirit* and prayer with the *mind* (1 Cor. 14:13-17).
Praying with the spirit may have been enriching for the prayer—but was unintelligible to others. Paul preferred to pray with
spirit *and* mind. Paul was bothered by his opponents' attempt to
separate the spirit and mind in prayer. Such a division reflected
an unhealthy dualism in the Corinthian view of human nature
and Christian piety.

Paul was neither a Greek philosopher nor a rationalist, but he
valued the human mind. He resisted the attempt of these pious
people to make prayer a special "spiritual" act unrelated to the
rest of life. To neglect the mind and pray with the spirit only
meant public worship was unintelligible to others (1 Cor. 14:16-
17).

Paul hinted that such "spiritual" prayer shows lack of regard
for others in the congregation. Paul's concern for praying with
the mind and the spirit reflects his view that the total person
should be oriented to the will of God. If prayer is neatly com-
partmentalized into a religious or spiritual part of life, the rest of
our actions may be contrary to the will of God. Frank Burns was
publicly very pious, but his private life was not consistent with
his prayers.

Earlier in 1 Corinthians Paul criticized people who assumed the spiritual and bodily dimensions of life were unrelated. These people argued they could do anything they wanted with their bodies (1 Cor. 6:12-13). Paul reminded them that any physical action was integrally related to life in the spirit. Indeed, they could honor God with their bodies (1 Cor. 6:19-20).[7]

In his letter to the Roman Christians, Paul echoed his concern that the total person be involved in worship. He told them "to present your bodies as a living sacrifice, holy and acceptable to God, which is your spiritual worship" (Rom. 12:1, RSV). The word translated "bodies" probably refers to the total person, not merely physical nature. The word translated "spiritual" could be rendered "logical" or "reasonable."

Paul was not separating mind from spirit or body. Our total selves can approach God, and our prayers reflect who we are. When we change the way we pray, then we begin to change who we are. Prayer changes our priorities. Commenting on the notion of persistence in prayer, Jennings noted, "To persist in prayer means that what we pray determines how we live."[8] If prayer were a pious act, isolated from the total person, it would not have such an impact on our identity. Understood as an act of the total person, prayer can transform our values, attitudes, and actions in the world.

Is Anybody There?

Prayer should be dialogue with the true God. Although the vast majority of Americans still claim to believe in God, it is not always clear that they agree on the character or nature of God. Indeed, some scholars argue that polytheism may be more popular than monotheism at the level of experience or real life.[9] If people perceive there to be many gods available, the issue of prayer becomes even more urgent. To whom or with whom are you talking when you pray? False prayer is dialogue with the wrong god.

Elijah, the early Hebrew prophet, asked the Hebrews this question. The Hebrews, partly under the influence of King Ahab and Queen Jezebel, had begun to worship Baal and Asherah, Canaanite deities. At Mount Carmel Elijah posed an exclusivistic either/or option: follow Yahweh or these pagan deities. Syncretism, a both/and approach to religion, was not an option for the Hebrews.

Elijah did not pose the issue in terms of the fine points of doctrine or morality; he focused on prayer. It may sound crude to sophisticated Americans to have a prayer contest, but Elijah at least wanted to make it clear to his fellow Hebrews that the prophets of Baal and Asherah were praying to a different god. The contest would determine which god really listened and responded to prayer (1 Kings 18:24).

Baal and Asherah, of course, did not respond to their prophets' prayers. Yahweh did answer Elijah's prayer, and the people acknowledged Yahweh as the true God. Presumably they had been reminded of the proper dialogue partner for prayer.

Some in our culture resist the notion that prayer is talking with God. If we defined prayer as private meditation or a therapeutic act of self-help or self-hypnosis, prayer would be more tolerable.[10] Many today are willing to accept prayer as a private, subjective act. The only standards for evaluating such "prayer" seem to be the sincerity or the subjective state of the pray-er. The "objective" partner in the dialogue, real or imaginary, is unimportant.

One frequent theme in the *Peanuts* comic strip is Linus' hope that the Great Pumpkin will visit his pumpkin patch on Halloween. Linus misses trick or treating each Halloween as he patiently sits with his pumpkins. According to Linus, the Great Pumpkin will visit the most sincere pumpkin patch. Assuming there is no Great Pumpkin, Linus' sincerity is obviously futile. Sincerity is important in human relations and in prayer, but it does not make up for the absence of the Great Pumpkin.

Elijah's contest on Mount Carmel is a clear rejection of this total reliance on sincerity. When the pagan prophets prayed to Baal, Elijah never questioned their sincerity. He encouraged them to pray louder, but Elijah's satire was primarily directed to the "object" of their prayers, Baal. The pagan prophets demonstrated their sincerity by shouting louder and cutting themselves. The writer noted, "But there was no response, no one answered, no one paid attention" (1 Kings 18:29). When Elijah prayed to Yahweh, God's answer was quick, obvious, dramatic.

The difference in these pray-ers was not sincerity or some other subjective factor. The real difference was the god to whom prayer was offered. The popular movie *Close Encounters of the Third Kind* was advertised with the theme "We are not alone." Elijah was not alone. He prayed to the God who was real and responded. His sincere trust in God was important, but the existence of that God was even more fundamental. The prophets of Baal and Asherah, like many contemporary pray-ers, should ask, "Is anybody there?"

Prayer is talking with *God*, not just any god. Sincerity is not enough; Christian prayer involves the total person addressing the right audience—God. Paul Tillich popularized the concept of "ultimate concern" to refer both to the subjective and objective aspects of faith. Faith is both infinite passion *and* passion for the infinite. Idolatry is having an ultimate concern for a finite object. The inevitable consequence of such idolatry, Tillich suggests, is disappointment, as persons realize they have mistakenly worshiped the finite rather than the infinite.[11]

Eventually, if Tillich is correct, the idolater will realize the futility of such a practice. By contrast, genuine Christian prayer involves the total person praying to the genuine God, who can really hear and respond to those prayers.

Lord, Teach Us to Pray

If prayer is a conversation with God, then a specific human being or community must be talking with a specific God. Prayer does not occur in a spiritual world lifted out of the real world of everyday experience. The fact that I am a middle-aged, white, male, married, Baptist college professor certainly affects my prayers. Even more important, however, is the identity of the God to whom I pray. As a Christian my understanding of God determines or shapes my prayers.

Jesus' early disciples noticed his practice of prayer and asked him to teach them to pray (Luke 11:1). Jesus' response has become known as the Lord's Prayer or the Model Prayer (Luke 11:2-4; Matthew 6:9-13). In later chapters we will use the petitions of the Model Prayer as our guide to understanding the essential components of Christian prayer. Our study will not be limited to that text, but the Lord's Prayer is important as Jesus' specific response to the question of how to pray.

If we want to develop a truly Christian view of prayer, we must pay attention to these words of Jesus. The total witness of Scripture will shape our discussion, but the Model Prayer will be central. A study of prayers in the Old Testament would help us recover the theocentric (God-centered) perspective as a corrective to much of the anthropocentric (human-centered) perspective of our culture.[12] Focusing on the Model Prayer helps us develop a distinctively Christocentric (Christ-centered) understanding of prayer.

Prayer is part of a distinctively Christian response to narcissism. Interacting with the petitions of the Lord's Prayer will heighten our awareness of the essential message of the Christian faith and the tension between Christ and Narcissus. Focusing on the Model Prayer should also help us be more aware of the difficulty of living in and responding to a narcissistic culture.

2

Why Pray?

What is the use of praying? What will prayer do for me? Such questions are typical in our pragmatic, consumer-oriented culture. Christians ask these questions because they feel the allure of narcissism, and non-Christians ask them of us. How do Christians answer them?

A lot of pray-ers are foxhole pray-ers. They get along fine without God until a crisis develops, then they turn to God. Although the foxhole pray-ers may at the time feel totally sincere they may change their minds about the necessity of God or prayer when the crisis is over.

Father Mulcahy, the Roman Catholic priest on the "M*A*S*H" television series, once dealt with a foxhole pray-er. The wounded soldier had made a promise to God as he waited for medical attention. Now that he was recuperating, he wondered if God would hold him to the promise he had made in his foxhole. Mulcahy assured him God would understand his change of mind.

Jacob was a foxhole pray-er. Having cheated his brother Esau twice, he ran for his life. Stopping to rest for the night, he encountered God. God promised to care for Jacob and repeated the promises he had made to Jacob's father, Isaac. Although he was a scoundrel, Jacob recognized the presence of God and re-named the place Bethel, "house of God" (Gen. 28:19).

Desperate, running for his life, Jacob was glad to have God on his side. This encounter with God had not, however, instantane-ously made Jacob a saint. He had always operated on a pragmat-ic, self-centered level of morality. His name meant "supplanter," which suggests someone who tries to squeeze in front of some-one else in a line of people (Gen. 25:26). When Jacob met God at Bethel, he told God that *if* God would take care of him, *then* he would acknowledge him (Gen. 28:21). Jacob made his loyalty to God dependent on God protecting him.

Jacob was a typical twentieth-century bargain shopper. If God would offer a quality product with a lifetime guarantee, then Ja-cob would buy. Jacob's attitude toward God and prayer prevails today. What can I gain by praying? In this chapter we will exam-ine prayer in light of two problems: prayer as *monologue* and prayer with *wrong motives*. Then we will see how these two prob-lems emerge in a self-centered culture.

Mirror, Mirror on the Wall

Mirror, mirror on the wall,
Who is the fairest of us all?

This question was asked by the wicked stepmother in the chil-dren's story "Snow White and the Seven Dwarfs." As long as the voice from the mirror responded that the stepmother was the prettiest woman in the land, she was happy. People who spend a lot of time primping in front of a mirror are often considered vain or self-centered. They are usually more interested in a monologue than a dialogue, because they are the most interest-ing or important person they know.

When my teenage daughter talks on the phone, I assume she is carrying on a genuine conversation with another person. Until video phones become affordable, I won't be able to see the other person, but I trust there is a partner in the dialogue. Prayer is closer to my daughter's telephone conversation than the step-mother's encounter with the mirror.

Jesus illustrated how tempting it is to transform prayer from a dialogue with God into a mere monologue in his comparison of two pray-ers, a Pharisee and a tax collector (Luke 18:9-14). Both went to the temple in Jerusalem to pray, but their attitudes toward prayer were different.

The Pharisee is one of the most obnoxious, arrogant people in the Bible. Although he seems to be praying to God, he is really concerned only about his accomplishments. A clue to this man's understanding of prayer is in some of the old manuscripts of Luke 18:11. "The Pharisee stood up and prayed about himself . . ." is an accurate translation. Some of the old manuscripts, however, say he "prayed to himself . . ." (NIV text notes). The Pharisee was really talking to himself about himself! He was not talking with God. He could have saved his energy in going to the temple. A mirror would have done him as much good.

In Greek mythology Narcissus was a handsome youth who was fascinated with his reflection in a pool of water. I do not know of any record that he prayed to himself, but certainly he could count as the patron saint of mirror watchers and monologue pray-ers.

Introspection and soul-searching are admirable and have their place in the life of prayer, but narcissism is a dangerous preoccupation with yourself. Narcissism is a self-righteous attitude that blinds you to your own faults and causes you to be judgmental toward others. Luke tells us that Jesus directed this parable of the Pharisee and the tax collector to "some who were confident of their own righteousness and looked down on everybody else" (Luke 18:9).

What Do You Want?

The fellows I teach with often go to a neighborhood doughnut shop. I like to dignify these breaks as departmental conferences or interdisciplinary discussions, but they are really just coffee breaks. One of my colleagues consistently tries to resist the temptation to eat some pastry. Often he will buy a pastry and ask me, "Do you want half of this?"

My standard reply is, "No, I don't need it."

Of course, I always take half of what he offers! We've had this conversation so many times it has become a ritual. At first he jokingly accused me of lying when I said "No" but took some of the pastry. I explained that I was distinguishing two words, *want* and *need*. He had used the word *want*, and I had replied with the word *need*. Certainly I *wanted* pastry, but I did not *need* it.

If our prayers are to be genuinely Christian, we must pray to the right *audience* and with the right *agenda*. We've already seen some problems of praying to the wrong audience. Elijah taunted the prophets of Baal and Asherah for praying to a god who could not or would not answer. Jesus noted the danger of praying to oneself as the Pharisee did. True prayer is a conversation with the right partner, the God revealed in Jesus.

When we pray to the right audience, we must also have the right agenda. We can clarify our agendas by considering a question Jesus posed to two of John the Baptist's disciples. Jesus noticed the two men and asked, "What do you want?" (John 1:38). Jesus was probing for their expectations about their own lives as well as the Messiah. John the Baptist had already pointed to Jesus as the "Lamb of God" (John 1:29, 36), but Jesus knew the value of asking a straightforward question.

Throughout his public ministry Jesus encountered people whose agendas did not match his. A most vivid example is the feeding of the five thousand. The crowd had followed Jesus because of his signs and miracles (John 6:2). When the people grew hungry, Jesus multiplied the boy's sack lunch and fed the people.

The crowd, impressed, "intended to come and make him king by force" (John 6:15). Here was a clear clash between what they wanted and what they needed. The crowd wanted a king, but they needed Jesus. The presence of Roman soldiers was a constant reminder to the Jews that they were not politically free. A dominant aspect of the messianic hope was that the Messiah would reestablish the nation as a free state. Jesus was the Messiah but had a different understanding of his ministry.

When the crowd pursued Jesus, he pointed out that they followed him because they had full stomachs. They had seen the miracle but did not understand it as a sign pointing to God (John 6:26, 30-33). The full stomachs they wanted were not what they needed—which was the bread of God. They wanted the wrong kind of wonder bread. Although Jesus understood their deeper, spiritual need, he had been willing to start where they were. He ministered to their physical desire, then tried to show them their real need.

We often approach God with our felt needs or desires. During the course of our dialogue we begin to discern our real needs. The encounter with God through prayer can change our priorities and lives. Here prayer is often in tension with the agenda set by contemporary culture. Much media advertising addresses felt rather than real needs. We need nutritious meals, but some advertising suggests we really "need" a certain food sold at a certain store.

Some advertising is pitched to children. A young child might think she needs to buy a new toy because she has seen television present it in an appealing way. Sometimes when she finally gets the toy and its newness wears off she realizes she did not really need the toy after all.

In genuine prayer we are challenged to clarify our wants and needs. In other words, we can approach God with our questions and concerns, realizing that sometimes we are asking the wrong questions or have the wrong agenda. Our popular culture inclines us to debate the merits of wheat bread, rye bread, and so on, but Jesus urges us to try the bread of life (John 6:35).

If prayer can cause a reevaluation of our priorities, then for some people the gospel must be bad news before it is good news. If we pray asking, "What's in it for me?" we will be disappointed. God hears our self-centered request and may answer by asking, "Do you really need that?"

A few years ago I took my car to an automobile repair shop for a cheap front-end alignment. Following my wife's advice, I had carefully cut out the newspaper's discount coupon to guarantee the advertised price. Then came the bad news. Instead of a simple alignment, my front-end needed a major overhaul.

When the shock wore off, I realized the bad news was really good news. Tinkering with the front-end would not have solved my problem. I had gone to the garage with a simple request and got more than I asked for! I did not get what I wanted, but I got what I needed.

Prayer can be like that. We bring our superficial requests and shallow needs, and God offers us more than we ever imagined. Moving from felt need to real need can be painful, but the result is good news.

C. S. Lewis compared a life-changing encounter with God to a child visiting a dentist. The child wanted immediate relief from the pain of a toothache. He was reluctant to visit the dentist because he would want to do more than stop the toothache. God is like the dentist. You might want divine help with one sin or problem, and "he will give you the full treatment."[1]

Truly Christian prayer means praying to the right audience and following the right agenda. In the next section we will see how narcissism encourages the wrong attitude toward prayer.

Prayer in an Age of Self-Centeredness

Should Doctors Play God? Who Should Play God? Come, Let Us Play God. Such book titles may be overly sensational, but they highlight the intense contemporary debate over recent developments in medical science.

Bioethics, a relatively new science, may give us a clue to the basic values of contemporary culture. Bioethics is the branch of ethics that deals with the general issues of "birth, death, human nature, and the quality of life."[2] It addresses such issues as euthanasia, abortion, genetic engineering, and behavior modification.

To some bioethics is merely an exotic, specialized field of research. To others bioethics represents the worst expression of human arrogance. This second group argues that state of the art technology enables us to control our destiny in a totally self-centered way. Without taking sides, we can recognize the danger of self-centeredness in this aspect of contemporary life. Many people want to use power in a self-centered way.

Several analysts of contemporary American culture have suggested that our narcissism has deepened in recent years. Our culture often highlights personal satisfaction to the neglect of social concern. Topics such as self-actualization, self-help, and self-assertiveness are popular. We live in the "me generation."

For example, Christopher Lasch described American society as "the culture of narcissism." After the political activism of the

1960s, Americans retreated to "purely personal preoccupa-tions."[3] Many Americans became convinced there were no polit-ical solutions to social problems and focused on themselves.

Psychoanalyst Aaron Stern discussed the dangers of narcis-sism in *Me: The Narcissistic American*. He argued that all of us are narcissists from birth. The infant "enters the world with an om-nipotent illusion of total self-fulfillment."[4] We can learn how to love others, said Stern, and limit our narcissism.

Daniel Yankelovich pursued a similar line of thought in his study of the American search for self-fulfillment. Yankelovich suggested that the concern for self-fulfillment from the late 1960s to the early 1980s was partly a reaction to the earlier ethic of self-denial dominant in this country. The ethic of self-fulfillment was basically an ethic of duty to self. Books such as *Looking Out for # 1, Self-Creation*, and *Pulling Your Own Strings* re-flected this trend to narcissism or self-absorption.

Yankelovich saw signs, however, that the preoccupation with self-actualization was being replaced by an ethic of commit-ment.[5] This new ethic avoided the extremes of self-denial and me-first thinking.

More recently Robert Bellah and others have investigated the tension between individualism and commitment in American society. In *Habits of the Heart*, these authors focused on the impact of individualism in several areas of American life, including poli-tics and family life.[6]

Individualism has always been an important factor in Ameri-can life. These studies by Lasch, Stern, Yankelovich, and others point, however, to an intensification of individualism and con-sequent narcissism.

How should Christians respond to a narcissistic culture? What place is there for Christian prayer in an age of self-centeredness? The temptation is to oversimplify and turn the discussion into an either/or confrontation. Our analysis of Christian prayer is real-ly a case study of the perennial Christ and culture issue.

The traditional Christ and culture issue has been outlined in terms of several typologies. For the sake of simplicity, a spec-trum proposed by Robert Webber will be adequate. Webber pin-pointed three types or models: the separational, the identificational, and the transformational.[7]

The separational model stresses withdrawal from non-Christian culture (Anabaptists). The identificational model advocates participation in culture (some Lutherans, contemporary civil religion). The transformational model highlights the possibility of change in culture in human history (Augustine, Calvin, and liberation theology). Although Webber is especially concerned with evangelical social responsibility, this brief summary of his typology reminds us that historically there has not been just one Christian response to culture.

Our task is not to choose one model and advocate it. If American culture is narcissistic, however, then it is in tension with the Christian faith in general and Christian prayer in particular. One goal of this study is to explore the relationship of Christ and culture without setting up a false dichotomy. Frequently the discussion becomes polarized between the cultured despisers of religion and the religious despisers of culture.[8]

The former group includes people who are so committed to the narcissistic lifestyle that the Christian faith is unappealing. The notion of self-denial is totally meaningless or irrelevant to them. The latter group argues that contemporary culture is totally anti-Christian.

Ideally both groups would benefit from the study of the Christ and culture issue in regard to prayer. The cultured despisers of religion can learn that, even with the language of self-denial, Christians are not commanded to be doormats or wimps. Christian faith does not demand that we deny culture. The religious despisers of culture can learn that culture is not intrinsically evil. Perhaps, as one author put it, *Your God Is Alive and Well and Appearing in Popular Culture*. Christians may need to learn that God is not trapped behind the walls of their religious institutions.

Throughout this study one of the primary sources of examples of narcissism will be popular culture, including those films, television, and comic strips which graphically summarize the values and beliefs of a culture. Tillich once suggested that "religion is the substance of culture, culture is the form of religion."[9] Nelson noted, "Popular culture is to what most Americans believe as worship services are to what the members of institutional religions believe."[10] Contrasting a theology of Christian prayer with a theology of popular culture helps highlight the tension between Christ and Narcissus.

The Profit of Prayer

While I was browsing in a Christian bookstore, I saw a section entitled "Self-help." The section included some intriguing books, but I was puzzled by the title "Self-help." Do Christians really practice self-help? Do we really try to solve our problems with human resources alone? Would total self-reliance reflect our narcissistic culture better than the Christian faith?

Narcissists pray-ers often want specific things for themselves. They have a specific, self-centered agenda. Narcissistic pray-ers, like children anticipating Christmas, address God only when they have a wish-list of items to be provided by God. If narcissists have everything they want, they have no reason to pray. The contemporary narcissist, like the people described in Job 21:15, asks "What would we gain by praying?"

Near Christmas my two daughters always make a wish-list. They write down things friends and relatives could give them for Christmas. They're often easy to shop for because there is so much they want. If they had everything, however, they would be hard to shop for. The narcissistic pray-er either approaches God with a lengthy shopping list *or* sees no need for God.

A better view of prayer was captured by a cartoonist. A little girl prays, "I'm not asking for anything in particular, but you could surprise me." The little girl may be selfish but at least she has no shopping list. If we approach God in a spirit of openness, what do we "gain" from prayer?

Jesus' Model Prayer suggests at least five types of gain. First, we gain a deeper relationship with God as our Father. Second, we gain a sense of priority and purpose for our lives as we understand our place in God's kingdom. Third, we gain a new appreciation and gratitude for what God has provided. Fourth, we learn how to confess our sins and experience God's forgiveness. Fifth, we gain a realistic appraisal of the problems of life and how God sustains us through them.

3

Beyond God the Father?

How do you usually address God when you pray? Most of the time I begin "Our Father." Having memorized the "Lord's Prayer" early in life, that form of address seems natural and theologically sound.

A few years ago, however, I was asked to pray in a worship service on Mother's Day. When I began my prayer with my typical words, I suddenly realized that some in the audience either might see some humor in my talking to the heavenly "Father" on a day we were honoring mothers or might even take offense at my use of "Father."[1]

In recent years feminists have questioned the exclusive use of masculine terms such as Father to describe God. How can we address God without falling into male chauvinism? Certainly most Christians who use the term "Father" do not consciously intend to be sexist, but Christian feminists correctly note the danger of sexist language about God.[2]

Although the question of God's gender is crucial, our concern here is the more general one of understanding as clearly as possible the God to whom we address prayers. Jesus began the Model Prayer with "Our Father in heaven, hallowed be your name" (Matt. 6:9).

Our basic image or picture of God will affect our overall understanding of prayer. In one cartoon a minister, trying to avoid any language that might offend some, addressed God as the great "To Whom It May Concern." That kind of reference to God, however, will be offensive to many who feel comfortable with the traditional language for God. In this chapter we will explore a Christian understanding of God. Without attempting a complete doctrine of God, we will sketch some of the major characteristics of the God affirmed by Christians.

Are You Praying to a God Who Cannot Save?

In the ancient world the issue was typically not whether or not God existed but whose God was most powerful. Almost everyone, at least in the ancient Near East, believed in some deity. The debate was close to the child's claim, "My dad is stronger than yours!" When Elijah, for example, met the prophets of Baal and Asherah at Mount Carmel, he never directly denied the existence of those pagan gods. Rather, he demonstrated that they were impotent (1 Kings 18) and that Yahweh was the true God.

When the Hebrews were defeated by the Babylonians and entered the period of the Exile, they felt that their God had lost a battle as well. Isaiah reminded them that the pagan gods were mere idols; the true God was Yahweh, who would eventually liberate them. "Ignorant are those who carry about idols of wood, who pray to gods that cannot save" (Isa. 45:20). Praying to such gods is an exercise in futility because the only God who can save or help us is Yahweh.

When we turn to the late twentieth century, however, the issue for many is whether or not God exists. The evidence for God's existence does not seem so clear.[3] To illustrate the contemporary situation, one philosopher told a parable about two people, a believer and a skeptic, who found a clearing in the forest.[4] The believer thought a gardener cared for the plot of land, but the skeptic noticed only the weeds. Both saw the same evidence but reached different conclusions.

John Hick has proposed eschatological verification as a possible resolution to this ambiguity. If two travelers disagree on whether the road is leading to the Celestial City, the issue remains unresolved until they round the last corner. When the Celestial City appears, it will be obvious one was right.[5]

Others today actively deny the existence of God. A few years ago an atheist wrote to advice columnist Ann Landers, demanding that she quit pushing religion. Religion is a crutch, the writer insisted, for the weak. "Such nonsense is for weaklings and idiots who are unable to think for themselves or accept responsibility for their own actions."[6]

Many contemporary people experience the absence rather than the presence of God. Peter Hodgson notes two major reasons for this experience: contemporary secularism and radical evil.[7] That is, contemporary life seems understandable without recourse to the transcendent, or the God-hypothesis. And the problem of suffering seems to disprove the existence of God.

Although narcissists are not necessarily card-carrying atheists, they might agree with Ann Landers' correspondent. For them life is best lived without the restrictions of religion or the emotional need for God. Many narcissists are closer to an atheism of *presumption* than an atheism of *conclusion*.[8] Presumptive atheists presume or assume that there is no God. At the least, God is not relevant to them. Their lives can be full and meaningful without belief in God. As a character in the movie *Crimes and Misdemeanors* sees it, God is a luxury we don't need. More militant atheists may try to disprove God's existence logically.

In this chapter we will address three issues. First, we will look at contemporary rivals to belief in the biblical God. Second, we will examine major attributes or characteristics of God. Third, we will note the importance of the Trinity for our understanding of God. In the following chapter we will then turn to the relation of the Christian view of God to praise as a type of prayer.

Your God Is Too Small

How big is your God? When I listen to little children describe God, I'm reminded how much my own view of God has changed across the years. When I was a child, God was often indistinguishable from Santa Claus. I knew God was invisible, and I had never seen Santa Claus either. Somehow Santa Claus could be everywhere at once, at least when delivering presents on Christmas Eve. Most important, God and Santa Claus were judges of moral behavior. Like God, Santa Claus had a list of people and their deeds.

To which God do you pray? Although atheism is a serious rival to the Christian faith, false understandings of God are also dangerous. "Christianity's most virulent opponent has always been superstition rather than atheism; false gods are far worse than no god at all."[9]

J. B. Phillips devoted part of *Your God Is Too Small* to images or concepts of God that are limited or "small."[10] The unreal gods included God as resident policeman, parental hangover, heavenly bosom, and projected image. All these unreal gods are distortions of the biblical portrayal of God.

What kind of God do you believe in? Although Christians try to develop their doctrine of God primarily from the Bible other images of God permeate our culture. Several studies have explored the images of God available in popular culture.[11] Some of these images of God might seem compatible with Christianity, but some are serious rivals to the biblical view of God. We will look briefly at some of the major views of God popular today, using illustrations from motion pictures.[12] We will consider deism, pantheism, dualism, and agnosticism.

1. Some people want a *deistic* God who leaves them alone. When the movie *Oh, God* first appeared, some Christians thought its portrayal of God was scandalous. George Burns as God? When "God" approached John Denver, Denver was naturally surprised, later Denver's family and friends were predictably skeptical about his alleged dealings with God. Eventually theologians and ministers tried to investigate George Burns' identity. Could he prove he was really God?

The basic image of God in *Oh, God* is deistic. Based on the Latin word for God, *deus*, traditional deism perceives God as distant and aloof from human history, a watchmaker God or an absentee landlord. God made the world like a watch, wound it up, and left it running. In strict deism, God would not interfere in the course of human history. In the movie, however, that pattern is broken by George Burns visiting John Denver and trying to help straighten out the mess humans had created.

Some narcissists might accept a deistic view of God, since such a God would not interfere in their lives with miracles or morality. An absentee landlord God would be so far removed from the everyday events of life as to be, for all practical purposes, nonexistent. This God would be real but not relevant. The deistic view of God was current among the Epicureans in the ancient world. For Epicurus the gods were real but unconcerned about human affairs.[13]

2. For other people, *pantheism* makes more sense. If deists typically stress God as transcendent and distant, pantheists emphasize God as immanent and present. Like deism, pantheism is an ancient viewpoint that has been revitalized periodically.

In its simplest form pantheism affirms that all (*pan*) is God (*theos*) and stresses the immanence of God. Some Christians see pantheism in movies such as *The Dark Crystal*. In this fantasy movie the major conflict is between two groups, a peaceful, mystical group and the evil Skeksis. When the missing piece of the crystal is restored, a strange transformation occurs—the two groups merge into one. Good and evil, light and dark are temporary. Unity is eternal. Such an emphasis is typical of pantheistic mysticism.[14] Being absorbed into God's being, for example, elevates one beyond the normal boundaries of good and evil.

Narcissists might find pantheism appealing because they could consider themselves divine. The boundary between Creator and creature would blur or disappear. A narcissist wanting to control his or her own life can affirm that God is in me (or is me!), which is as convenient as saying God does not worry about me (deism).

3. Attractive to some people is the portrayal of life as a constant struggle between good and evil. Obviously war movies have always emphasized conflict between opposing forces. The religious view that echoes this image of struggle is *dualism*. Dualistic theology suggests that two ultimate principles or gods are in conflict. Good and evil battle for control of the universe.

Monster or horror movies come close to exemplifying dualistic thought even when there is no explicit reference to God. Movies that stress a supernatural dimension, such as *Poltergeist* or *The Exorcist*, come close to traditional dualism. Although in most of these movies the "good guys" eventually triumph, the central image is one of conflict or struggle.

The prevalence of crime and violence in contemporary society makes dualism attractive. Narcissists, who look out for their own welfare above all, may especially identify with the conflict mentality of dualistic thought. If life is primarily a struggle for dominance, the narcissist wants to come out on top. Surviving and succeeding motivate the narcissist to use any means to triumph in life's struggle.

4. *Agnosticism* is another attitude current in popular culture. Deists, pantheists, or dualists probably have wrestled with the God question and reached a firm conclusion about God's reality and relevance for them. Agnostics also confront the question of God's existence but believe there is no clear way to decide yes or no. An agnostic does not know whether or not God exists.

Such an attitude seems close to the opinion of a psychiatrist in the movie *Agnes of God*. When a dead baby is found in a convent, a psychiatrist is appointed by the court to investigate the mother's conception and the child's death. A young nun had apparently conceived and delivered the child under mysterious circumstances. The psychiatrist initially assumes there can be no supernatural dimension to the child's conception, but at the end of the movie she seems willing to look beyond the naturalistic explanation and allow for an element of mystery.

Narcissists are normally so preoccupied with themselves that they see no need to trouble themselves with such issues as the reality of God. Agnosticism seems plausible since the evidence is vague and debatable. Why not just get on with life rather than arguing about speculative issues such as God's existence?

These views (deism, pantheism, dualism, agnosticism) are merely examples of popular ways of looking at God. Narcissists might identify with any of these views as long as their basic concern, themselves, is undisturbed.

In light of the biblical understanding of God, however, all these views are inadequate. These gods are too small. God is transcendent but not distant and detached as in deism. God is immanent but not identified completely with us as in pantheism. Life does include some struggle between good and evil, but the conflict is not perpetual as in dualism. Doubt may arise for the devout as well as for the agnostic—but we can choose to live by the faith that God does exist.

God Is Great, God Is Good

Having glanced at a few of the rivals to Christianity, we turn to a Christian understanding of God. A full doctrine of God is not possible here, but some features of a doctrine of God are essential to our theology of prayer.[15] As a teacher of theology I realize how difficult it is to speak meaningfully about God in a short space. Robert Capon's advice is sound.

> The job of the theologian is not to unscrew the inscrutable. His highest hope is not that his analogies will unveil absolute truth; only that they will make as little trouble as possible.[16]

Ultimately God is mysterious and transcends human language, but the Bible reveals to us much to affirm about God in contrast to rival views mentioned in the last section.

Besides Bible study, our view of God is shaped through personal and family experiences. "God is great, God is good, let us thank him for our food . . ." is the beginning of one of my earliest experiences with prayer and God. This children's prayer before a meal has much good theology packed into it! The greatness and goodness of God could be used as the umbrella categories for a very full discussion of God's attributes.[17]

Jesus was not delivering a formal theology lecture when he taught his disciples the Model Prayer. But the opening lines, like the child's mealtime prayer, summarize important themes. "Our Father in heaven, hallowed be your name" (Matt. 6:9). In other words, God is our heavenly Father, and he deserves our respect.

"Our Father in heaven" points both to God's greatness and goodness. Assuming you have a good human father, you will think of God the Father in positive terms. Yet God is not exactly like your earthly father. "Father" is a good comparison for God, yet there is no strict identity between earthly fathers and the heavenly Father. Such language is metaphorical or comparative. God is and is not like a human father.[18]

Because God loves and cares for us like a human father, it is meaningful to call God our Father. By referring to God as our Father in heaven, however, Jesus reminds us not to limit God to our human perception of fatherhood. God loves us like a parent, but God is not male. Indeed, some biblical texts use feminine imagery for God (Isa. 42:14; Luke 15:8-10). Some psychological critics of Christianity suggest that the image of God as father is a projection of our human conception of fatherhood onto God. Paul, however, suggests that human fatherhood is derived ultimately from divine fatherhood (Eph. 3:14-15, NIV note).

Scholars have noted that Jesus on occasion used a special term for "father"—*abba* (Mark 14:36). Abba is an Aramaic term suggesting great familiarity and intimacy that could be translated "Daddy" or "Papa." Jesus was apparently the first Jew to use such a term for God.[19] The Jews of the Old Testament were familiar with the notion of God as father (Hos. 11:1-3; Mal. 2:10), but they did not refer to God in the familiar sense used by Jesus.

Paul told Christians that they had the right and privilege to address God as Abba (Rom. 8:15; Gal. 4:6). Paul emphasized, however, that we are adopted into the family of God (Gal. 4:5). The prophet Ezekiel had used a similar image for the relation of God to the Hebrews (Ezek. 16:1-7). As one credit card company notes, "Membership has its privileges," and children of God can call on God in prayer as their divine parent.

Lest we become too chummy with God, however, Jesus instructed his followers that God's name must be "hallowed." To hallow is to honor or respect. Although God is good, God is also great and deserves our respect and honor. God's name reflects God's nature.

Jesus' instruction probably reflects the Hebrew concern about the significance of God's name. The name Yahweh was typically not spoken out of reverence for God. Much as we use nicknames to capture a prominent physical characteristic ("Redtop") or a personality trait ("Honest Abe"), the Jews saw names as a clue to your identity. To hallow God's name means to give God the respect God deserves.

How would you finish this statement? God is _____. Although the Bible does not stress dictionary-type definitions of God, several passages could be used to answer this question.

Perhaps the most popular answer is "God is love" (1 John 4:8, 16). Certainly God's love for us is central to both testaments. God's love can be compared to several types of human love. C. S. Lewis noted four common analogies: the love an artist feels for an artifact, the love of a man for his beast, a father's love for a son, and a man's love for his wife.[20]

Other scriptural answers to the fill-in-the-blank question include God is light (1 John 1:5), God is faithful (1 Cor. 1:9), and God is spirit (John 4:24). One of my favorite descriptions of God is "I am compassionate" (Exod. 22:27b, RSV). The word "compassion" is close to terms such as empathy and sympathy. God feels with us. God understands our suffering and identifies with our situation. God is not distant and detached as in deism. Rather, God knows our situation and responds to our need.[21]

Although this definition approach to God's nature has scriptural precedents, much of the biblical witness to God comes in the form of narrative. Rather than defining God or offering simple propositions about God's nature, the writers of Scripture often told stories of God's actions in history.

Jesus, for example, frequently used parables to present his understanding of God. Luke 15 records three such parables that characterized God as a shepherd looking for one lost sheep out of 100, a woman looking for one lost coin out of 10, and a father waiting for his lost (prodigal) son. God is like a shepherd, a woman, and a father. All three images are metaphorical yet illuminate the loving character of God.

How should we pray to God as heavenly Father? A narcissist might see God as a "soft touch" who will give anything he or she wants. As we will see in the sixth chapter, we can make requests to God, but the narcissist sees petition as the only relevant type of prayer. Praise is an alien type of prayer to the narcissist.

The Strong Name
Several years ago I began to end many of my prayers with the phrase "in the strong name of Jesus." My primary motivation was to remind myself of the Hebrew emphasis on the link between name and nature mentioned earlier. One danger of such a phrase, however, is that the name *Jesus* might be perceived in a

magical, superstitious sense. A narcissist or an immature Christian might think that God will automatically grant all requests simply because the word Jesus is being used.

In his discussion with the disciples in the upper room, Jesus repeatedly referred to prayer in his name (John 14:13-14; 15:16; 16:23-24). He emphasized that the disciples would use his name because of their strong, personal relationship with him. For example, "If you abide in me, and my words abide in you, ask whatever you will, and it shall be done for you" (John 15:7, RSV). Rather than offering his followers a blank check in prayer, Jesus was emphasizing that prayer in his name was a natural aspect of their relationship to him and God the Father.

Another danger with my phrase, "the strong name of Jesus," is that it only mentions one of the three members of the Trinity. I was not intentionally ignoring the Father and the Holy Spirit, but a listener's theological antennae might have started to quiver! Distinctively Christian prayer is always addressed to the Triune God revealed in Scripture, even when only one is mentioned explicitly. God is Father, Son, and Spirit.

The doctrine of the Trinity may make some readers nervous. Few of us can explain the doctrine well, so we tend to avoid it. One writer even called it "the guilt-producing doctrine"![22] Others react to the doctrine with sincere puzzlement. Millard Erickson quotes the witticism,

> Try to explain it, and you'll lose your mind;
> But try to deny it, and you'll lose your soul.[23]

Likewise, Shirley Guthrie notes the importance of the Trinity: "It is the uniquely Christian answer to the question who God is, the answer that distinguishes the Christian understanding of God from that of other religious or philosophical views."[24] Convinced the Trinity is essential to mainstream Christianity, we wrestle with how to make sense of God being three in one.

Many Christians have their favorite analogies or illustrations of how three can be one. My theology students are familiar with the children's book I use that compares an apple to the Trinity.[25] Just as an apple has a peel, flesh, and a core, so God is Father, Son, and Holy Spirit. A good friend uses his three roles as husband, father, and teacher. These analogies and others have some value although they do not remove the mystery which shrouds the Trinity.

One element of the orthodox doctrine of the Trinity often overlooked in the search for adequate analogies is the relation of the eternal Trinity to the economic Trinity.[26] This traditional jargon may be alien to some, but the concern behind it is legitimate.

The economic Trinity refers to the historical revelation of God as triune. The word *economic* comes from the Greek words for home (*oikos*) and rule or order (*nomos*). "Economics" originally meant the orderly management of a home, something like household finance. In theology, economic was used to reflect the orderly disclosure of God's triune nature. The eternal Trinity refers to the eternal nature of God as triune. What is revealed (economic Trinity) is what God really is (eternal Trinity).

Affirming this close link between the economic Trinity and eternal Trinity will help us avoid two dangers. First, we can avoid seeing God as a committee of three separate individuals. Although one of the three may seem more prominent at a certain point in history, all three are eternally real.

Second, we can avoid assuming that the inner essence of God differs from God's revelation. In the movie *The Wizard of Oz* Dorothy and her friends finally have the chance to see the great wizard. They discover, however, that an ordinary man is pretending to be the great wizard by projecting an awesome image on a screen. He tells them to ignore the man behind the curtain. He's that man and wants them to see only the image of the wizard on the screen. Some people believe that God is not really triune. The real God, they say, is one; the threeness is an illusion.

To which God do we pray? Although our culture has a strong secular flavor to it, there are also many rival gods claiming our attention. Are we praying to the true God who can save?

4

Prayer That Breaks the Bonds of Self-Love

Who is the most self-centered, egotistical person you know? My first example comes from "M*A*S*H," for several years my favorite TV show. Set in the Korean War in the early 1950s, the show dealt with the doctors and nurses of a Mobile Army Surgical Hospital. The most narcissistic person on the show was Colonel Charles Emerson Winchester, who was an outstanding surgeon—and knew it!

My other choice is Stephanie from the Bob Newhart show that aired in the late 1980s. While Winchester seems more true to life, Stephanie is obviously a caricature of a narcissist. Although she works as a maid and waitress in Newhart's inn, her high society background continually surfaces.

Comic strips also are populated with self-centered people. In *Peanuts* Linus comments, "It says here that the world revolves around the sun once a year. . . ."

Lucy replies, "The world revolves around the sun? Are you sure? I thought it revolved around me!"

We moved from a geocentric (earth-centered) worldview to a

heliocentric (sun-centered) worldview with the rise of modern science. Now our culture may be experiencing an increasingly egocentric (self-centered) worldview.

Excessive self-love is not new, however. In the first century John noted the trouble caused by Diotrephes, "who loves to be first" (3 John 9). Speaking of the "last days" Paul said people would become lovers of themselves rather than lovers of the good or lovers of God (2 Tim. 3:1-5).

This self-love is associated with love of money, love of pleasure, arrogance, conceit, and other negative character traits. Self-centeredness might have peaks and valleys in human history, but it is always a potential rival to the Christocentric life.

It's Hard to Be Humble

Extreme forms of egotism are easy to identify in comic strips and television programs. Most Christians, however, encounter the temptation to narcissism in much more subtle forms. Richard Foster tells of attending a conference where he received lots of praise. After twenty-four hours of compliments, he told his wife they had to leave before he started to believe it! A few pages later he commented, "Narcissism is excessive self-love, and it is the dominant mood of our age."[1]

When narcissism is in the air, we must learn how to respond to it critically and creatively. Christians are not immune to the influence of narcissism. Although we live in the world, our values and beliefs are not to be worldly (John 17:15-16).

Our dreams may be a clue to the influence of narcissism on our values and beliefs. In the children's story "The Dream," Toad dreamed he was on stage and his friend Frog was in the audience.[2] Toad played the piano and asked Frog if he could play that well.

"No," Frog said. Frog began to look smaller to Toad. Toad walked on a high wire and later danced, but Frog could do none of this. Eventually Frog was so small Toad could not find him.

Joseph's dreams resemble Toad's. Joseph dreamed that he would rise to prominence and his family members would bow down to him (Gen. 37:5-11). When he reported the dreams, his brothers became jealous. Although the dreams did come true when Joseph rose to power in Egypt, his brothers undoubtedly perceived Joseph as an egotist of the first order.

Narcissism is currently popular among analysts of culture as a label for self-centeredness, but theologians have generally used "pride" as their term for this aspect of the human predicament. Many theologians have cited pride as the basic human sin. One influential twentieth-century advocate of this view, Reinhold Niebuhr, suggested that humans are created as finite and free.[3] When tempted, humans often exploit their freedom while denying or ignoring their finitude. They tend to "play God" in their lives rather than acknowledging their limited freedom.

Pride was included in the church's list of the seven deadly sins. Recently sociologists and psychologists have begun to see the value of this traditional list of vices for understanding human behavior. Although pride is a perennial human attitude, narcissism may be especially prominent in our generation. Henry Fairlie noted, "The self-love of Pride is more unbridled than at any other time."[4]

If we are like Toad in dreaming we are the "star" on stage in the spotlight, what are the consequences? Narcissism can impact our lives in terms of four relationships. First, narcissism affects *our relation to God*. If the narcissist wants to be center stage in life, then obviously God is pushed off-stage or becomes a bit player in the drama of life.

If the true God is not being honored, then the human being plays God. Adam and Eve displaced God by deciding that they would set their own rules for life in the garden. Rather than recognizing the boundaries set by God, they claimed the knowledge of good and evil. The knowledge they gained by eating the fruit of the tree was not conscience or a sense of morality, for God had already given them an awareness of certain moral standards. The knowledge of good and evil was actually the presumed right to determine what they would call good or evil.

To emphasize that we are creatures does not mean we have to "put down" human nature. Some evangelical Christians are so concerned to emphasize our sinfulness that we forget we are created in the image of God. I recall as a child singing about being a worm in the old version of the popular hymn "At the Cross."[5]

We will explore the topic of human sinfulness in chapter five, but here we need to recall that God created us in God's image. One reason for the emergence of narcissism in contemporary culture may be a reaction against the extremely negative view of human nature popularized in some Christian theology. The universality of sin is a strong evangelical theme, but the fact that we are "fearfully and wonderfully made" (Ps. 139:14) should be accented as well.

For example, the hymn "I Surrender All" is theologically valid as a reaffirmation of God's sovereignty, but an extreme emphasis on self-denial opens the door to narcissism. Emphasis on the image of God reminds us that self-esteem and self-denial are complementary in the Christian life.[6]

We must avoid too quickly judging each other's narcissism. Psychologists note that the infant has legitimate narcissistic needs that must be met if the child is to mature into a healthy adult. Some of our adult narcissistic tendencies come from unmet childhood needs. When this is true, we do not need criticism of our self-absorption. We need to be loved deeply enough to learn to love ourselves and move beyond our unquenchable thirst for attention and nurture.

A second impact of narcissism is on *our relationship to other people*. If we adopt a belief system and value system like narcissism, then other people are valuable to us only if they can help us be important. When Toad dreamed he was on stage, his friend Frog grew smaller and smaller. Presumably Toad needed Frog as an audience to notice how well he played the piano.

Narcissism creates an attitude of envy and jealousy. The narcissist is often afraid that someone else will gain the honor or praise he or she wants. Saul, for example, became jealous of David after he killed Goliath. Saul noted that the women sang, "Saul has slain his thousands, and David his tens of thousands" (1 Sam. 18:7). Irritated at the unfavorable comparison, Saul became jealous of David. If he had been less narcissistic, Saul might have been glad for David's victory over the Philistines.

Revenge may be another expression of narcissism. If an egotist has been genuinely wronged or feels wronged, the urge may be to get even. Joseph's brothers apparently expected him to seek revenge after their father Jacob died. Since the brothers had seen Joseph as a self-centered teenager, they expected him to try to get even later. But Joseph did not play God. He forgave his brothers for selling him into slavery. He told them, "Don't be afraid. Am I in the place of God?" (Gen. 50:19). A true narcissist would have wanted to take God's place and seek revenge.

The manipulation or exploitation of other people is basic to narcissism. In one comic strip, Sarge tells Beetle Bailey, "Beetle, pick up that mess!"

Beetle retorts, "Oh, you act like you're God or something."

Sarge's reply reflects this theme of manipulation. "Listen, if I were God you wouldn't have to obey me. You wouldn't be in my outfit."

To a narcissist other people are pawns to be moved on a chess board.

A related expression of narcissism is libertinism. Narcissists believe they are free to do what they want as long as it pleases them. When a professional athlete was asked if he was overly ambitious, he said, "I don't think so. I'm here on earth to please me, and that would please me."[7]

Paul encountered a similar attitude among Christians at Corinth. They argued that in light of the freedom offered by Christ, they could do whatever they wanted. The specific issue confronting the Corinthian church was whether to eat meat that had been offered to idols. The libertines argued that they could eat anything they wanted. Paul said such an attitude showed lack of concern for weaker, less liberated Christians. Christian love should guide liberty. Near the end of his discussion, Paul notes, "Nobody should seek his own good, but the good of others" (1 Cor. 10:24).

Narcissism can cause a lack of sensitivity to other people. Like a horse wearing blinders, we may be unaware of the needs or responses of others because we are too busy focusing on our own. A narcissist like Cain might ask, "Am I my brother's keeper?" (Gen. 4:9), but the Christian attitude is "Do not think of yourself more highly than you ought" (Rom. 12:3).

Narcissism can begin with a reasonable self-concern, but it often leads to a sense of self-sufficiency that results in a denial of our need for community with others. It refuses to recognize our obligation for community with other people.[8]

A third consequence of narcissism involves *our relation to the physical world*. Although God told Adam and Eve to have dominion over the world (Gen. 1:26), some have exercised domination and exploitation rather than Christian stewardship. Pollution, for example, is not a wise use of our environment.

Dr. Seuss' children's story, *The Lorax*, illustrates the tendency to harm the physical world for profit. An aggressive, greedy man cuts down all the trees to make a product nobody really needs. Eventually all of the trees are gone, but one seed is left. Will someone plant the seed and give the trees another chance? The word *ecology* comes from the Greek word for home (*oikos*) and points to our need to treat the physical world as our home.[9]

A fourth consequence of narcissism is *its impact on ourselves*. One theologian identified examples of the effects of sin on the sinner: enslavement, flight from reality, denial of sin, self-deceit, insensitivity, self-centeredness, and restlessness.[10] Interestingly, several of these point to the preoccupation with self that characterizes narcissism.

All these expressions of narcissism are based on an attitude epitomized in the country and western song that says, "It's hard to be humble when you're perfect in every way." Although few people claim to be perfect, many find it hard to be humble. Our culture tends to see humility as vice rather than virtue. Humble people are perceived by narcissists to be doormats or wimps. Humble people haven't achieved anything, narcissists claim, so they have no reason to boast.

A key misunderstanding here is that Christian humility is not the same as a lack of accomplishment or a low self-esteem. Biblical people who were humble were often great achievers. Moses, for example, led the Hebrews out of Egyptian captivity in the greatest event in Hebrew history, the Exodus, but he was "more humble than anyone else on the face of the earth" (Num. 12:3).

The apostle Paul was a brilliant thinker, writer, and speaker, but he realized that all of his accomplishments were trash when compared to his new relation to Christ (Phil. 3:3-10). Paul stressed that Jesus was the role model for true humility. Humility entails concern for the interests of others (Phil. 2:3-4).

The supreme example of this self-sacrificial attitude is Jesus, who "humbled himself and became obedient to death" (Phil. 2:8). Although the eternal Son was equal to God the Father, he did not cling to that status but freely took the form of a servant.

Authentic humility respects our legitimate need to be affirmed and involves how we relate to others rather than culti-vating a view of ourselves as insignificant. Whose interests do we put first? Are we willing to give credit where credit is due? If we reach some goal in business, music, school, athletics, or church, we can legitimately feel a sense of accomplishment with-out becoming egotistical or obnoxious.

The apostle Paul achieved much as a Christian missionary, yet he always realized that "by the grace of God I am what I am" (1 Cor. 15:10). Acknowledging God's role in his life did not di-minish the achievements, but Paul was willing to give God ulti-mate credit.

I Call You Friends

What is your favorite description of God? The Bible uses many images or word pictures for God, each accenting a differ-ent dimension of God. For example, God is Lord, King, Master, the Good Shepherd, Liberator, Husband, Father, and Rock.

Recently some theologians have focused attention on the con-cept of God as Friend. I grew up singing about Jesus as my best Friend, but the idea of God as Friend was new to me. Jesus told his disciples he would no longer call them servants but friends (John 15:13-15). James reminded us that Abraham was known as God's friend (James 2:23).

Although *friend* is not a dominant scriptural image of God, it should be taken seriously, especially given narcissist objections to Christianity.[11] Narcissists may dislike acknowledging God in their lives because God is seen as a foe or rival. Who's in charge, me or some authoritarian God? Many people seem to believe that following God means a loss of dignity and self-worth.

Perhaps the friend image will reassure them that God does not have to be a rival. George Buttrick, in his classic study, de-fined prayer as "friendship with God."[12] Seeing God as divine

Friend as well as Father would help a narcissist overcome the image of God as a rival.

The use of the language of liberation to describe God, like the language of friendship, helps correct the misunderstanding of God as oppressor. The apostle Paul frequently used the language of slavery to describe the relation between God and his people. Slavery was a widely accepted institution in the first century. On occasion, however, Paul stressed that our relation to God was not enslaving in the oppressive sense of limiting our personal freedom. Our relation to God is that of a son rather than a slave (Gal. 3:26—4:7). Seeing God as Friend and Father is liberating rather than enslaving.

God *or* freedom seems to many a fundamental choice today. Many contemporary liberation movements reject authoritarianism and assume that Christianity is anti-freedom. In the name of self-respect or personal dignity, many people have rejected God, or at least a common stereotype of God. The biblical God is actually pro-freedom and accents human dignity.[13] Still, this God is to be praised. Narcissists often sense God is a competitor because they want the world to revolve around them.

In an age that promotes self-love, Christians are called to praise a majestic God. An essential part of prayer is the acknowledgment of God. Adoration includes reverence and awe in the presence of God. But it does not mean we must deny we are God's creatures, created in God's image, or that we have excelled in some arena of life. We can accept praise for a job well done without becoming a narcissist.

In a comic strip, a character notices a sign on the wall that says, "If you don't swallow it, it can't hurt you."

He asks, "Food?"

Another person replies, "Praise."

If we become enamored with praise, we lose our perspective. Seeking praise from others or praising ourselves can be dangerous to our spiritual health.

Praise of God is fundamental to Christian prayer. Praise is a natural, spontaneous response to the presence of God our Friend and Father. Praise flows from a sense of abundance rather than a sense of duty, from enjoying and not only enduring God.[14]

5

Whose Kingdom Is It, Anyway?

What do movies like *Places in the Heart*, *Tucker*, and *Gorillas in the Mist* have in common? They all celebrate the dedication of heroes and heroines to a cause. Whether the cause is saving the family farm, building an innovative automobile, or protecting an endangered species, the cause is deemed worthy of heroic effort. Some may experience such movies as inspiring because they challenge the viewer to respond heroically to whatever difficulties or adversities they face. Whether the task or project is voluntarily accepted or thrust upon the person, a deep commitment of personal energy and resources is an appropriate response.

In the Model Prayer, Jesus taught his disciples to pray, "Thy kingdom come. Thy will be done, on earth as it is in heaven" (Matt. 6:10, RSV). Scholars debate the fine points of interpreting these lines, but most agree that the kingdom of God was central to the teaching of Jesus, especially in the synoptic Gospels. Most also agree that the kingdom of God refers to the reign or rule of God in human lives, not a geographical or national kingdom.[1]

What does "kingdom" language mean today? Kings and kingdoms are not usually part of our ordinary experience. Are there contemporary images or terms that could serve as functional equivalents? Here are three examples of efforts to translate kingdom of God language into contemporary idiom.

First, *project* might substitute for *kingdom*. William Dyrness suggested understanding Christianity as the project of God. "That is, Christianity tells us what God has done, is doing and will do in the world, and what we must do in response. . . ."[2]

The language of project reminds me of a line from the Broadway musical *South Pacific*. One character says, "I like projects, don't you?" If the kingdom is God's project, then Christians should like it and join in enthusiastically. Project has the advantage of pointing to an organized effort to meet a goal.

Second, Clarence Jordan used "God Movement" instead of "kingdom of God" in his Cotton Patch translation of the gospels.[3] Jordan's personal involvement in the civil rights movement made the language of *movement* especially meaningful to him. Certainly contemporary social and political movements have a kind of family resemblance to the kingdom concept.

In addition, movement highlights the communal or corporate dimension of the kingdom image. Since some evangelicals tend to overemphasize the individual's relation to God, movement imagery reminds us that the kingdom is inherently social.

Third, Wes Seeliger suggests the *wagon train* as a model for Christianity. Authentic Christianity is the journey of God's wagon train into the unknown, with God as trail boss and Jesus as scout. Western or pioneer theology captures the spirit of adventure and risk-taking involved in genuine faith. Seeliger contrasts pioneer theology with settler theology or institutional Christianity, with its preoccupation with safety and security.[4]

Jesus' Model Prayer instructs us to pray for the coming of God's kingdom and that God's will be done.[5] American culture, however, frequently inclines us to pray for ourselves. Are these two attitudes reconcilable? Our concern in this chapter is to focus on the tension between the priority of the kingdom of God for Christians and the narcissist's preoccupation with self.

Narcissism encourages an acquisitive, consumer-oriented lifestyle. In a comic strip, Cathy debates whether she would want a child. "My house is for me! My money's all for me! My whole life revolves around me, and I love that! Me, me, me! . . . I'm torn between wanting to have one and wanting to be one."

Many Christians feel the dilemma. Advertisements and other aspects of popular culture encourage us to look out for ourselves first, yet our Christian faith stresses seeking the kingdom of God. In the old children's game "King of the Mountain," one child stakes out a position on a hill or a piece of playground equipment and tries to fight off others who want to be king. For the narcissist, life becomes a struggle to stay on top.

Jesus told his disciples, "Seek first his kingdom and his righteousness . . ." (Matt. 6:33, RSV). Seeking the kingdom of God and praying for its arrival are complementary aspects of the Christian life. They both require us to establish and follow distinctively Christian values. As we feel pulled in many directions by the claims of culture and the Christian faith, we need a clear sense of who we are and where we are going.

A few years ago the *New Yorker* magazine cover pictured a businessman with captions depicting all the claims on his life (corporate responsibility, family, work ethic, Judeo-Christian tradition).[6] How does a Christian decide what to do? James, anticipating this dilemma, encouraged us to possess purity of heart rather than a divided mind (James 4:8). Soren Kierkegaard developed this thought in his devotional classic, *Purity of Heart Is to Will One Thing*.[7] Our lives will have a clear focus when we make the kingdom of God the guiding light for our decision-making.

Cooperating with God

A narcissist might respond to this emphasis on the kingdom of God by saying that Christians are being encouraged to be weaklings or wimps. The whole notion of God as King means, according to narcissists, that Christians are weak, servile, impotent beings. Christians, the narcissist could charge, are passive supporters of the status quo. "Let go and let God" means there is no room for human creativity or autonomy. Contemporary narcissists could applaud the parody of the Christian hymn, "Rise up, O Men of God":

> Sit down, O men of God,
> His Kingdom He will bring
> Whenever it may please His will;
> You cannot do a thing![8]

Such a critique of Christianity is partly right. Christians have sometimes uncritically supported the status quo. When H. Richard Niebuhr cited the major criticisms of Christianity across the centuries, he included otherworldiness and quietism as two of the three perennial charges.[9]

One underlying problem seems to be the critic's misunderstanding of God's sovereignty as manipulation or coercion. If God is the sovereign Lord of the universe, are we mere puppets? Is a God who is all-powerful also the cause of everything? Christians typically believe God can do anything but not necessarily that God has done everything that occurs in human history.[10]

Some Christians realize that although God may not need our help, God has chosen to welcome our cooperation. Marie Balter, for example, was able to rebuild her life after spending twenty years in a mental institution. Misdiagnosed and treated for a problem she did not have, she eventually was released and joined mainstream society. A devout Christian, she said, "Nobody does this alone. I don't feel responsible for my success. I feel I'm responsible for cooperating with God."[11]

God's self-emptying in the incarnation (Phil. 2:7) is a clue to God's relationship to the world. It at least points to God's willingness to limit God's dealings with the world.[12] Some Christians see God's sovereignty on the model of a mother cat carrying her kitten by the neck. Others see God as the monkey whose baby clings to her as the mother travels. The mother is in charge in either model, but the monkey analogy allows for human participation rather than passivity.[13]

The notion of our cooperating with God might seem strange to some, but Paul used the image of being a fellow worker with God in his description of his ministry (1 Cor. 3:6-9). Paul had planted, Apollos watered, and God gave the growth. "For we are God's fellow workers" (1 Cor. 3:9a).

God's sovereignty is not threatened by seeing Christians as co-workers. God sets the agenda and invites us to join in the work. Harvey Cox once compared the action of God in the world to a floating crap game. The Christian's task is to find the action and join in![14]

Christians sometimes struggle with cooperating with God because God is not doing what we expected. For example, John the Baptist announced the coming of the Messiah but later had second thoughts about Jesus' agenda. From jail, John sent messengers to ask Jesus, "Are you he who is to come, or shall we look for another?" (Luke 7:19, RSV). Jesus' response was to confirm his own agenda through examples. He pointed to his miracles and preaching to the poor. When Jesus commissioned the twelve, he gave them instructions that mirrored what he had been doing (Matt. 10).

Some Christians have been so sensitive to the criticism of social conservatism that they have moved to the extreme of talking as if the kingdom of God will be ushered in strictly through human activity. The "social gospel" movement at the turn of the century was often accused of this excess. Some see this danger in some of the liberation theologies of the last half of this century.[15] Ideally Christians will remember that the kingdom is God's—yet God called us to cooperate in God's work on earth.

Praying that God's kingdom will arrive does not require a total separation between divine sovereignty and human activity. Thomas Merton, for example, was able to balance the contemplative life and social concern in his own experience. He frequently spoke and wrote on the great social issues of our day, but he never forgot that he was a Trappist monk.

When a group of seminary students visited Merton at the monastery, one was suspicious that Merton had forgotten the concerns of the real world. Didn't Merton feel he should be doing something, the student asked? Merton replied that he believed in intercessory prayer![16]

Like Merton, we need to learn a balance between the contemplative life and the active life. Men and women of God do not have to sit down and passively wait for God's kingdom to arrive.

Honoring God with Lips and Life

The word *transparent* can refer to windows or people. A transparent person is someone whose inside and outside are consistent. What you see is what you get. An opaque person, by contrast, is someone whose interior and external lives diverge.

Consistency between appearance and reality is also known as integrity. In recent years we have seen an integrity crisis in American religious and political life. Revelations of immoral behavior have shaken our confidence in some of our leaders. Like Paul, our leaders need to be able to say, "Our sole defense, our only weapon, is a life of integrity" (2 Cor. 6:7, Phillips).

The ideal in God's kingdom is that we be transparent. Our beliefs and behavior should coincide. Jesus frequently warned against the danger of hypocrisy. For example, he criticized those who would say "Lord, Lord" but would not do the will of the Father (Matt. 7:21). He warned his disciples of the hypocrites who did not practice what they preached (Matt. 23:2-3). Citing the prophet Isaiah, he said hypocrites are the ones who "honor me with their lips, but their hearts are far from me" (Matt. 15:8).

Such warnings about hypocrisy remind us that life in the kingdom requires integrity. High quality movies frequently focus on people of integrity who stand up for their convictions despite opposition. *Chariots of Fire* told the story of Eric Liddell, a British Olympic runner in the 1920s who refused to compete on a Sunday because of religious convictions about the Sabbath.

Authentic Christianity reflects the values of the kingdom and is rooted in doing what Jesus expects. When Jesus compared the wise man and the foolish man as they built their homes, the key difference was their response to the words of Jesus. The wise man put the words into practice, but the foolish man ignored them (Matt. 7:24, 26). James echoed Jesus when he said we should be doers of the word, not merely listeners (James 1:22).

One reason we struggle with the integrity issue is our desire to be noticed or praised. Even if we are not card-carrying narcissists, always seeking the spotlight, we often fear being ignored. Jesus reminded us that even pious actions can be done for the wrong reasons, including drawing attention to ourselves. In the Sermon on the Mount, he dealt with the issue of motives for three traditional pious actions: giving alms, prayer, and fasting (Matt. 6:1-18). Jesus did not criticize these three actions but highlighted motive. In effect, Jesus said, Do not do these good deeds primarily to be noticed by other people (Matt. 6:1). Jesus' recurring emphasis is that we should seek to please the Father, not draw attention to ourselves.

Jesus offered the Lord's Prayer as a positive example after describing a self-centered pray-er. For the hypocrite who seeks to draw attention to himself as he prays Jesus recommends private, secret prayer (Matt. 6:5-6). Should all of our prayer be limited to our prayer "closet"? Does Jesus mean to eliminate all public prayer? Certainly we are familiar with public pray-ers who seem to be delivering an oration to impress a human audience rather than praying to God. Would Jesus discourage us from praying before a meal in a public cafeteria?

Many practice prayer before meals and do so without consciously drawing attention to their piety. Public prayer before meals can be both a witness to other diners that one is a believer and a sincere expression of gratitude for the food. But Jesus was concerned that public prayer could easily slip into a hypocritical display of religiosity. Does the prayer (lips) reflect the real values of the pray-er (life)?

This emphasis on the danger of seeking fame might prompt someone to ask, Is there anything wrong with wanting to be noticed? On the bulletin board outside my office I posted a newspaper headline, "Lifestyles of the Poor and Anonymous." Intended to parody the television series, "Lifestyles of the Rich and Famous," the headline sets up a false dichotomy—fame or anonymity. Must Christians be anonymous?

Jesus *was* concerned about our doing good deeds primarily to get praise. Certain activities are inherently public, however, and we cannot remain anonymous. If, for example, you are a Christian athlete or musician and excel, fame may be unavoidable. But a Christian athlete or musician committed to honoring God will cultivate humility. Eric Liddell in *Chariots of Fire* said God created him to run fast. When he ran, he felt God's pleasure.

Surely God expects members of the kingdom to excel with whatever talents or abilities they have. Making fame the goal of the activity, however, creates tension between loyalty to God and seeking the praise of people.

6

Prayer as Petition in an Age of Self-Assertiveness

In a comic strip the mother reminds her children to say their prayers at bedtime. After the "Amen," we see an angel in heaven next to an overworked computer labeled "Petitions." Not long after I saw that cartoon I noticed a book entitled, *God Is Not a Vending Machine . . . So Why Do We Pray Like He Is?*[1]

Both the cartoon and the book title point to the common perception that prayer is primarily asking for God to do something. Some Christians are so sensitive to this perception that they suggest asking is a primitive or childish form of prayer.[2] Real prayer, they argue, is meditation or contemplation, not asking. As the book title suggests, God is not a vending machine. The pray-er is not a consumer trying to buy a product.

A narcissist might have mixed feelings about prayer as asking for something. On the one hand, this kind of prayer implies that the pray-er is dependent on God. Critics of religion such as Freud and Marx have noted that religion can be a psychological crutch. Weak people turn to God; strong, mature people do not need God's help.[3]

The search for autonomy or independence in contemporary culture often meshes with the self-centeredness of the narcissist. According to conventional wisdom, a person who is dependent on others or lets them dominate is a wimp. A person who is assertive and aggressive is liberated. On the other hand, a narcissist might find petition the only appealing prayer. Prayer becomes the way to get what the narcissist wants. Praise and confession suggest focusing on God, but petition means getting!

In this chapter we will explore three aspects of the complex issue of prayer as asking. First, we will look at the scope of prayer. For whom should we pray? Second, how do we discern and enact the will of God? Third, why do we need to pray when God already knows what we need?

Can We Pray for John Wayne?

A few years ago a member of my Bible study asked, "Can we pray for John Wayne?" We normally had a time of prayer requests and prayer, so the question was not totally surprising. None of us knew John Wayne personally, but we knew he was ill. Somehow the request seemed odd.

As I've reflected on the question, I see it as a good example of a larger question: For whom should we pray? My class normally limited its prayer requests to people and situations we knew firsthand. Occasionally we might mention a political leader or the victims of disaster in another country. Predictably, we often prayed for me and mine.

Traditionally we divide prayer as asking into two categories: petitionary and intercessory. Petitionary prayer is asking God to do something for us individually. Intercessory prayer is asking God to do something for someone else. Narcissists would naturally assume petitionary prayer makes more sense simply because they stress anything that benefits them personally.

In this section we will focus on intercessory prayer. Imagine a bulls-eye with a series of concentric circles. The innermost circle represents your concern for yourself. The next circle represents your family. Each succeeding circle symbolizes a circle of concern such as friends, co-workers, American society, and planet earth. Perhaps one reason the prayer request for John Wayne was so surprising was that we jumped from the inner circles to a frequently ignored circle, public figures.

In Dr. Seuss' *Horton Hears a Who*, Horton the elephant hears a cry for help from a tiny civilization of Whos. No other jungle animals seem to hear the Whos, but Horton sets out to rescue them from danger. Despite ridicule, Horton perseveres. Christians should be alert to the cries of people like the Whos, especially when they are overlooked by other segments of society.

We are naturally more aware of human need closer to us, but we can cultivate sensitivity to the needs of the larger world. A danger for the contemporary church is that we expend all of our energy with self-preoccupation and self-perpetuation. Tony Campolo tells a parable of a visit to an oil refinery.[4] The tour guide pointed to the elaborate machinery for processing the oil. When asked about the shipping department, the tour guide said there was no shipping department. All the raw material was used to keep the refinery going! In prayer we need to avoid devoting all our energy to praying for ourselves and those close to us geographically and emotionally.

When Christians ask God to do something, their priorities should reflect God's. A life focused on God will mirror God's concerns. For example, a commentary on Habakkuk introduced me to the notion of God's *infracaninaphilia*. This strange term means love of the underdog.[5] God consistently takes the side of the poor and oppressed. The Bible frequently addresses the issues of poverty and hunger, but Christians often ignore these concerns unless personally involved.

Attending college during the heat of the civil rights movement of the 1960s, I became aware of the plight of blacks in this country. To me blacks had been invisible people.[6] I was blind to the situation of blacks until the civil rights movement forced me and many of us to confront the issue.

Jesus knew that we become preoccupied with issues that blind us to life's top priorities. In the Sermon on the Mount he urged the disciples not to worry or be anxious about food and clothing (Matt. 6:25-32). Their ultimate concern should be the kingdom of God. "But seek first his kingdom and his righteousness, and all these things will be given to you as well" (Matt. 6:33).

Jesus was not ruling out prudent concern for the physical ne-cessities of life but was warning against narrow preoccupation with such issues to the neglect of the kingdom of God.[7] Later Je-sus criticized the hypocrites for focusing attention on tithing spices while ignoring "the more important matters of the law—justice, mercy and faithfulness" (Matt. 23:23).

Our petitionary and intercessory prayers should echo God's concerns. Do we pray exclusively for ourselves and our close friends and relatives? Are we aware of the needs of others in the more remote concentric circles of concern? A truly Christian pray-er cultivates an awareness of the invisible people, the Whos of life, and prays for them as well. Such praying does not require total disregard for our own individual needs—but it may demand reevaluation of our prayer priorities.

Should my class pray for John Wayne? We did, but what did we ask God to do? Should we ask that God heal Wayne's illness or that God's will to be done? A fuller discussion will be provid-ed in the chapter on deliverance from evil, but a few comments are relevant here. Certainly the will of God at times is that we re-cover from physical disease. James, for example, instructed the early Christians to call the elders to pray for the sick (James 5:14-15). Paul, however, prayed for deliverance from his thorn in the flesh, and the thorn remained. Paul learned that even with this affliction God's grace was sufficient to sustain him (2 Cor. 12:7-10).

If genuinely attuned to the will of God and kingdom values, we will not ask God to do something out of character. As a child I knew my parents well enough that I did not ask them to do cer-tain things. Often I wanted something I knew they would con-sider frivolous or extravagant. Although initially I did not always appreciate their judgments, I later learned the wisdom of their values. The better we know God, the more likely we are to ask for what God can and will do. My class did pray for John Wayne, but he died. Our faith in intercessory prayer was not demol-ished, however, because we had prayed that God's will be done.

Where Two or Three Are Gathered in My Name

How do you determine the will of God? Is your decision-making done solo? Several years ago one of my college students came by to tell me he was dropping out of school. He had earlier dropped several courses, and I had sensed he would eventually drop the rest. When I asked how he reached this decision, he replied that he had prayed.

I then asked if he had talked to anyone else. Obviously nervous about my questions, he admitted he had talked to one friend. I did not try to dissuade him from quitting school, but I tried to explore with him his decision-making process. My impression was that he had made this decision and many others in a very individualistic way. He had not come to me, his faculty adviser, for advice. He apparently did not feel comfortable seeking advice from anyone else. His pattern was to pray about whatever issues he faced.

American culture has traditionally encouraged individualism, but narcissism pushes the notion of individualism to an extreme. A narcissist might say, "I am my best self when I am on my own." Harold Kushner summarized the narcissist's creed: "I am not here to worry about your needs and I don't expect you to worry about mine. It's every man for himself."[8] For a narcissist, decision-making is a lonely, solitary venture. On rare occasions the decision-maker might seek advice, but basically decisions are private issues.

One common interpretation of the Bible emphasizes the one-on-one relationship between God and the individual. We often highlight the stories of the solitary saint struggling with the will of God. Because of dramatic events such as Moses at the burning bush or Saul on the road to Damascus, we begin to assume that all Christian decision-making is done solo.

Although our relationship to God is in many ways private and personal, much of Scripture highlights the corporate or communal dimension of decision-making. For example, Jesus used the kingdom of God concept extensively in his teaching. The kingdom image is basically a social one, with several people committed to a common leader and a common goal. Paul referred to the church as the body of Christ, highlighting the interdependence of the members of the body (1 Cor. 12:12-31).

In the book of Acts, Luke stressed the sharing and cooperation of the Jerusalem Christians (Acts 2:42-47; 4:32-35). The Christian life is envisioned as a community of believers, a partnership, not a lonely vigil. Jesus promised his followers that "where two or three are gathered in my name, there am I in the midst of them" (Matt. 18:20, RSV). Jesus was giving instructions on how to deal with a sinner in the community (Matt. 18:15-20). If a person sins against you, first make a private approach. If repentance does not follow, then the community becomes involved. Jesus promises to be present as the group decides how to handle this situation.

How might a group of Christians be involved in decision-making? Some have a negative impression of the quality of group deliberations. A camel, we've been told, was a horse designed by a committee! In traditions that stress the priesthood of the believer, discussion of the role of the group sounds threatening. Certainly there are times the majority is wrong. Insightful, prophetic individuals can correct the errors of the group.

Nevertheless, the pooling of insights from the group can produce deepened understanding of God's will. Simply meeting together is not enough, of course. Jesus added the qualifier "in my name." The group discussion must be guided by kingdom values. Mere pooling of human opinion or preferences will not do.

Birch and Rasmussen have suggested three ways the community can positively influence decision-making. The church can serve as a shaper of moral identity, a bearer of moral tradition, and a community of moral deliberation.[9]

First, our basic identity is shaped by the local congregation to which we belong. Through explicit teaching and preaching we learn some basic Christian beliefs and values.

Second, a local church and a denomination develop a heritage of moral concern and wisdom. This moral tradition might change over the years, but the moral heritage should be taken seriously by individual Christians.

Third, the church can engage in moral deliberation. Churches often do creative seeking of God's will in committees and in business meetings. For example, when my local church discusses its annual budget, ideally it is trying to match its financial resources to kingdom values. Will we spend most of our money on ourselves, or will we exercise a Christian global consciousness?

Richard Foster notes the role of a "meeting for clearness" in decisions.[10] For example, a young couple might come to the community seeking advice about whether to marry. Foster acknowledges that decisions are finally made by individuals, but advice should be sought from wise counselors and be taken seriously.

Many of my students resisted Foster's suggestion that a church might speak to a couple's decision about marriage. Why? Perhaps these students have received inappropriate advice before or have observed incompetent groups. Or perhaps they have placed too high an emphasis on the individual. Their pietistic, free church background probably inclines them to extreme individualism. They might not be narcissists, but they overemphasize individual assessment of God's will.

As we become more aware of the need for a collective *discernment* of the will of God, perhaps we can also see the value of cooperation among Christians in *doing* the will of God. To cooperate with God's kingdom or project requires us to join with other Christians. Our individualistic culture values competition over cooperation in many arenas of life. Self-interest expresses itself in a competitive lifestyle. Self-identity and self-esteem seem based on the number of our achievements. Many young people are conditioned to believe that finishing second is as bad as being last. The only thing that counts is winning.

Christians realize that sometimes the value of the group transcends the individual. One scene in the movie *Star Trek II: The Wrath of Kahn* gave a secular equivalent to the biblical concept of sacrifice. To repair damage, Mr. Spock enters an area of the spaceship Enterprise contaminated with radiation. Knowing he will die, he explains his action by saying the need of the many outweighs the need of the few or the one.

Such a sentiment was for Caiaphas a shrewd political strategy, but it became a theological truth in the death of Jesus (John 11:50; 18:14). Caiaphas urged that Jesus be eliminated to restore peace to Jerusalem. The death of Jesus actually provided salvation from sins, not mere public tranquillity.

The values of working together and sacrificing for others rather than competing are clear in Scripture. Luke noted the sharing and cooperation in the church in Jerusalem. Rather than hoarding their possessions, many donated them to the church for the use of the needy (Acts 2:44-45; 4:32-37). Paul criticized the competitiveness and factionalism of the church at Corinth. Paul encouraged the Corinthians not to brag of their spiritual gifts but to reaffirm their interdependence as members of the body of Christ and work for "the common good" (1 Cor. 12:7).

When Christians work together, they can discern the will of God and make a concerted effort to accomplish that will. Individual Christians need not forsake personal piety and practice, but their prayers should acknowledge the wisdom of other Christians. Two heads may be better than one, especially when they confer in the name of Jesus.

God Already Knows Our Need

In C. S. Lewis' *The Magician's Nephew*, Polly and Digory are bothered by the lack of food. Fledge, the horse with whom they are traveling, has found plenty of grass to eat. But the children have nothing and are disgusted. When Fledge says that, if asked, Aslan would certainly have met their needs, Polly wonders if Aslan wouldn't know their needs without being asked. " 'I've no doubt he would,' said the Horse (still with his mouth full). 'But I've a sort of idea he likes to be asked.' "[11]

In Lewis' story Aslan the lion represents Christ, and the children are asking a question many raise. If God already knows our needs, why do we have to ask God to do something about them? Perhaps God could say to us, "Don't call me, I'll call you."

Jesus raised this when warning people against being verbose in our prayers. Some seemed to think lots of words might lead to more divine attention. "Do not be like them, for your Father knows what you need before you ask him" (Matt. 6:8, RSV). Since God knows everything, we do not pray to add to the divine data base or heal divine amnesia. Why then do we pray, asking for something to happen?

Do we hope to change God's mind? Most Christians affirm that God does not change (Mal. 3:6; James 1:17). The passages that trouble us, however, refer to God repenting or changing God's mind. When Amos, for example, began to have visions of divine judgment on the Hebrews, he prayed and God repented (Amos 7:1-6). Did God's mind really change?

Theologians have proposed several theories about such passages. Some suggest that divine repentance is an example of *anthropopathic* language—that is, humanlike feelings are attributed to God. God does not really change, but God's actions look to us like what we would do if we changed our minds. By contrast, some suggest that God's repentance actually referred to God's working out of a new stage of relating to the Hebrews. As long as the Hebrews rebelled, they deserved punishment. If they repented, the punishment would not come.[12]

Key to resolving this issue is God's relationship to time. A few years ago I was preaching for a friend who had flown to another state for a meeting. Early in the worship service my friend's trip was mentioned as a prayer request. About 7:00 p.m. we prayed for his safe arrival home. Later I learned that he had actually arrived in town before 7:00, and, fatigued, went to his home rather than joining our worship.

Through divine foreknowledge, God knew about our prayer before the plane trip occurred. There was nothing silly about praying for an event that had already happened. Although we affirm divine sovereignty of human history, our actions and prayers are known to God. On this issue, C. S. Lewis commented, "My free act contributes to the cosmic shape."[13] We did not change God's mind, but I believe our prayer was taken into account by God in shaping the course of history.

If prayer does not give new information to God, why ask anything? Lewis' story provides a clue. As Fledge the horse said about Aslan, perhaps God "likes to be asked." Prayer is fundamentally part of our overall relationship with God. Although God is the omnipotent, sovereign Lord of the universe, God does not normally invade our lives uninvited. As long as we choose to live our lives on our own strength and resources, God honors that decision.

To use a crude analogy, consider a traditional courtship in which the man is expected to propose marriage to the woman. The man might take a long time deciding whether he wants to propose to the woman. Or he may know he wants to marry her, but he is too timid to ask. For her, it was love at first sight, and she patiently waits for her suitor to propose. All along she knows she will say yes, but she waits to be asked. God's love for us means God often waits for us to ask, even though God already knows what we need. Only when we realize the need will we ask, and God will respond.

In our courtship analogy, we assumed the woman was willing to marry the young man once he proposed. In asking God to do something, however, we sometimes feel that God does not hear our requests or does not grant them. Jesus consistently emphasized that God is willing to answer our requests. God will respond to our asking, seeking, and knocking (Matt. 7:7-11).

Several times Jesus used a graphic compare-and-contrast style of teaching to reinforce the responsiveness of God. If a son asked for bread, the father would not give him a serpent (Matt. 7:9). In the parable of the man who had an unexpected guest late at night, Jesus emphasized that the sleepy neighbor would eventually get out of bed to help. Surely God is much better than the sleepy, grumpy neighbor (Luke 11:3-13).

Likewise, the parable of the judge who finally helps the widow illustrates the readiness of God to help us (Luke 18:1-8). God is not stingy in relationship to us. God is predisposed to answer our prayers. Still, God may want to be asked, since the asking is essential to the divine-human relationship.

Lest we think Jesus was giving his followers a blank check, he often reminded them this freedom to ask emerged within their relationship with the Father. In the Upper Room Jesus noted that the asking was rooted in this relationship (John 14:13-14; 15:7, 16; 16:23-24). If we abide in Christ and ask in his name, reflecting his priorities, God *will* hear and respond to our requests.

In this same session where he explains the privilege of asking, however, Jesus warns of the adversity his followers will face. They should not then expect to be delivered from all opposition. Encountering opposition would characterize loyalty to Jesus. When Jesus prayed for them, he asked not for their exemption from trouble but for God to sustain them in the trouble (John 17:15). As believers we are encouraged to bring our requests to God but are not promised we will get everything we want.[14]

Thank God It's Friday

How do you respond when you receive a gift? When I was a child, my parents expected me to write thank-you notes for presents I received. I usually did my duty, but my enthusiasm for the project depended on the nature of the gift. If I had received something I really wanted, such as a football or a bicycle, I had no difficulty writing my sincere appreciation. But if the gift were less desirable, such as clothes, then I often procrastinated. I knew gifts and gratitude were to be automatically linked, but I did not always feel grateful for some gifts.

In the movie *A Christmas Story* an elementary school age boy's heartfelt desire was to receive a Red Ryder BB gun for Christmas. Whenever he expressed this desire, he was told of its danger. "You'll shoot your eye out!" was the refrain from his mother, his schoolteacher, and even the department store Santa Claus.

On Christmas morning his hopes were dashed as he opened each present, because there was no BB gun. After all of the gifts were opened, his father pointed to a package hidden away. It was his BB gun. Although he had feigned appreciation for most of the other gifts, now he was truly grateful.

In this chapter we will examine the relationship between gifts from God and our gratitude for them. In the Model Prayer Jesus instructed his followers to pray, "Give us today our daily bread" (Matt. 6:11). Although the form of this line is a petition, we will look both at the plea for daily bread and our response to the granting of the request.

Is saying "Thank you, God" enough? What is the best way to express gratitude to God? How should this request for daily bread shape our values and beliefs about God and our lives in his kingdom? How can a Christian legitimately ask God for what he or she needs without becoming narcissistic.

Thank You God for Everything and Everyone

Probably the most common time for thanking God is a prayer before a meal. Even if gratitude is not part of our daily thinking, meals might prompt the familiar custom of saying "grace." When my children were younger, we taught them familiar prayers such as "God is great, God is good, let us thank him for our food. By his hand we all are fed, give us Lord our daily bread."

Later they began to voice their own prayers. My younger daughter, Karen, frequently uses the same words: "Thank you God for everything and everyone." Perhaps unconsciously she has condensed and modified another prayer my wife and I taught our children. "Thank you for the world so sweet. Thank you for the food we eat. Thank you for the birds that sing. Thank you God for everything."

Karen's prayer has at least one danger and two values to it. The danger is that the prayer is too sweeping and generic. The old chorus reminds us to count our blessings by naming them one by one. Being specific in itemizing our blessings would probably help us be more aware of our dependence on God. Thanking God for everything and everyone is equivalent to asking God to forgive us for our "sins" without naming them. Itemizing blessings (or sins) may be time consuming, but sometimes we need that activity as a helpful spiritual exercise. What exactly are you grateful for?

Karen's simple prayer also has two values. First, the prayer gives us a cosmic or comprehensive perspective on life. Thanking God for everything and everyone covers a lot of ground! Paul's advice to "give thanks in all circumstances" (1 Thess. 5:18) sounds the same theme. Gratitude is spontaneous when you have received a much-wanted gift, but some circumstances of life might make gratitude more difficult. Selective gratitude is more typical for most of us. We thank God for the good events and people of life but complain about the rest.

We will turn to the problem of suffering in life in chapter eleven, but here we need to recall that gratitude for all of life is essential to the Christian way of life. When John Claypool's daughter died of leukemia, he struggled with the reasons for her brief life. He rejected the approaches of unquestioning resignation and total intellectual understanding and affirmed gratitude.[1] Claypool concluded the most Christian approach was to see his daughter's life as a gift. He still hurt over the loss of his daughter but acknowledged that her life, indeed all life, is a gift from God which calls forth our gratitude.

The second value of my daughter's prayer is its reminder of the intimate link between God, the supreme source of all gifts, and the gifts themselves. James told the early Christians, "Every good and perfect gift is from above, coming down from the Father of the heavenly lights" (James 1:17). A self-centered person easily focuses on the gift rather than the giver.

In one television show a wounded white soldier says he will not accept a blood transfusion from a black person. The doctors darken his skin with iodine while he is asleep, then tell him he must have received blood from a black man. This superstitious racist believed he was becoming a black man. The clincher, however, comes when they tell him how the man who invented part of the process of preserving plasma died because he could not be admitted to a hospital in the United States. The inventor was black.

The wounded soldier appreciated the gift, the possibility of blood transfusion, but he did not appreciate the giver, the black man who invented the process. True gratitude should be a sincere response to both the gift and the giver.

The comic strip character Dennis the Menace once said before a meal, "Instead of giving thanks for our food, couldn't we just give God and Mom a big hand?" Dennis sensed, quite correctly, that both God and his mother had been involved in bringing the food to the table.

God is the ultimate source of all good gifts, but human beings are also involved as the penultimate agents of God's generosity. Saying grace before a meal is a helpful act of piety, but gratitude should not be the end of the process. Acknowledging the gift and the giver is important, but gratitude should result in our generosity as well. When Paul encouraged the church at Corinth to give to the offering for the Jerusalem church, he also pointed to the close relationship of giver, gift, gratitude, and generosity.

Jesus was rich, but he became poor in order for them to become rich (2 Cor. 8:9). The experience of grace through the new relationship with Jesus should motivate them to be generous in helping the struggling church in Jerusalem. He based his appeal on their gratitude for God's gift of his Son. "Thanks be to God for his indescribable gift!" (2 Cor. 9:15).

Death by Bread Alone

When Jesus told us to pray for daily bread, did he mean physical bread only, or did he include spiritual nourishment as well? In this section we will focus on this line from the Lord's Prayer as a further example of petitionary prayer, the type of prayer we investigated in chapter six. In that study we highlighted the need to pray in the right way for the right things. Here we ask what kind of "bread" we are to request.

Holy Materialism

For a long time *materialism* was a dirty word to me. Christians were to be concerned with the spiritual, not the physical. My view was partly shaped by my early religious experiences and partly by my culture. Growing up in a small, conservative church and a blue collar family, I tended to be suspicious of the wealthy, assuming that the less you had the more pious you were.

Occasionally someone I knew became successful in business and began to compromise their religious convictions. *See, you can't be spiritual and materialistic at the same time,* I thought to myself. Gradually, however, I began to realize that the Christian faith encourages a healthy appreciation for the physical world. A. M. Hunter, commenting on the daily bread petition in the Lord's Prayer, defended it as an expression of "holy materialism."[2]

The bread we are to request is ordinary, physical bread, not spiritual nourishment. William Temple's claim that Christianity is the most materialistic of the major religions also reminds us that Christianity is world-affirming rather than world-denying.[3] In general Temple recognized that Christianity affirmed the goodness of the world as created by God. By affirming the goodness of creation, the incarnation, and the resurrection of the dead, Christians reject any dismissal of the physical world as inherently evil.

In light of this world-affirming attitude, we will look now at three views of the meaning of the prayer for daily bread. All these views have been held by Christians in recent years, but the first two come dangerously close to the narcissist mind-set.

First, some people seem to revel in the physical and orient their lives to accumulating as many physical possessions as they can. Such an attitude appeared in Greek mythology in the story of King Midas. Midas became so enthralled with the beauty and value of gold that he wanted to get as much as possible. Similarly, Hagar the Horrible, a cartoon character, espoused the motto, "I got mine." His wife suggested that it should also say, "and heaven help the guy who tries to take it away."

The Hebrews' experience with manna reflects the temptation to hoard bread. One condition imposed by God was that they collect enough each day for the family's needs (Exod. 16:4). Some people hoarded more than one day's supply of manna, but the bread spoiled. Jesus' instruction about daily bread probably echoes this familiar story. Our request for bread is to be for what we genuinely need. To want more than we need is irresponsible.

Jesus' parable of the rich fool illustrates the tendency to become preoccupied with possessions (Luke 12:13-21). As he prospered, a farmer did not have enough room to store his crops. He decided to build bigger barns and live a life of leisure—only to have it all taken away. Jesus used the parable to warn against covetousness and greed. Clarence Jordan noted that God's pronunciation of judgment should be translated "This night *they* require thy soul of thee" (Luke 13:20).[4] His possessions possessed him!

How much is enough? How much bread do we really need? Most families can find a way to spend all of the money or bread that comes in. A bumper sticker says, "My money talks to me (but it only knows how to say good-bye)."

Langdon Gilkey learned how selfish good, civilized people can be while interred in a Japanese camp during World War II. The American Red Cross delivered about 1,500 parcels of food and supplies to Shantung Compound, where Americans and persons of several other nationalities were being kept under guard. Rather than allowing the parcels to be distributed to all the prisoners, the Americans argued that each American should get several parcels apiece.

The selfishness of the Americans infuriated the other prisoners. The ensuing controversy baffled the Japanese. Gilkey summarized his conclusion with words from Bertolt Brecht's *The Threepenny Opera*:

> For even saintly folk will act like sinners
> Unless they have their customary dinners.[5]

A second attitude toward bread and the whole physical world is asceticism, or extreme self-denial. Certainly self-denial is a strong biblical theme in the sense of avoiding narcissism, but asceticism can become excessive. Even Jesus and his disciples encountered some criticism for not following a strict ascetic lifestyle. Followers of John the Baptist noted that they and the Pharisees fasted, but Jesus' disciples did not. Why? Jesus responded by comparing his followers with wedding guests that celebrate his presence as the bridegroom (Matt. 9:14-15). Jesus attended enough dinner parties and other festive occasions that he gained a reputation as a glutton and a drunkard (Matt. 11:16-19).

Asceticism is sometimes built on a dualistic separation of the physical and the spiritual into two distinct compartments. Dualists can then argue that the physical is bad and the spiritual is good. Such thinking easily leads to rejection of the physical, and to an extreme otherworldliness. Paul, for example, responded to some dualists who encouraged abstinence from marriage and certain foods. Paul reaffirmed the goodness of creation in the context of thanksgiving to God (1 Tim. 4:3-5).

On the surface the ascetic attitude looks like it would be exempt from narcissism, but such extreme self-denial can become a self-centered way of life. The ascetic may focus attention on self and forget that, for Jesus, self-denial is part of a larger perspective. Jesus encouraged self-denial in the context of commitment to the kingdom of God. Three times when predicting his suffering and death, Jesus mentioned self-denial (Mark 8: 31-38; 9:30-37; 10:32-45). Each time the disciples seem to ignore or misunderstand his words.

The self to be denied is the narcissistic one. Preoccupation with self is idolatry that rejects the priorities of God's kingdom. When Jesus urged a supreme loyalty to the kingdom of God, he recognized that concerns for food, shelter, and clothing would then have their appropriate place (Matt. 6:25-33). Worry or anxiety about these physical necessities is alleviated whenever disciples place their ultimate loyalty in God. Christians can exercise prudent concern about necessities such as food and clothing without becoming narcissistic.

Self-denial can be narcissistic when, for example, a pious act such as fasting is done for an ulterior motive. Jesus warned against fasting when the motive is to be noticed by other people rather than to cultivate a spiritual life (Matt. 6:16-18).

Isaiah expressed a similar concern about fasting in his day. Although the people practiced fasting, they still exploited their workers (Isa. 58:3-4). Self-denial is essential when self conflicts with kingdom values. Self-denial should not, however, become an opportunity for feeling holier-than-thou.

The third and best attitude toward bread is simplicity. We should seek bread adequate and necessary for each day. Living in a culture that is generally affluent, this is difficult. So much is available that we feel like someone in a cafeteria line. The temptation is to put more on our plate than we need.

In "The Girls" comic strip, a woman prays before a full table, "And please give me the strength to resist the bounty you have provided." Praying for ability to resist the abundance reflects the affluence of our country and would not be a concern in many countries.

When Paul encouraged the Corinthian Christians to be generous in contributing to the offering to the Jerusalem church, he noted that equality was the goal (2 Cor. 8:13-15). He did not expect one group to sacrifice so another would flourish. The ideal was for the abundance of one church to be shared. Such advice about stewardship might seem odd to many in our culture, where possession is a major concern.

Adopting a simple lifestyle would be painful for many of us, but it is closer to the intent of prayer for daily bread than either preoccupation with possessions or extreme asceticism. In recent years authors such as Richard Foster and Ron Sider have helped recover this vision of a simple life for many Christians.

Foster cited simplicity as one of several spiritual disciplines in *Celebration of Discipline*. He expanded his discussion in *Freedom of Simplicity*.[6] Foster contrasts simplicity with the materialism of this age and legalistic asceticism.

Ron Sider develops a similar emphasis in the context of world hunger and poverty.[7] Christians need to adopt a lifestyle that will enable them to address these major social issues.

The experience of Koheleth in the Old Testament illustrates the value of a modest life-style. After experimenting with a variety of ways to find meaning in life, his conclusion was that everything was meaningless (Eccles. 2:17). Rather than despairing, however, he affirmed that some activities are what God wants us to do in life. "A man can do nothing better than to eat and drink and find satisfaction in his work. This too, I see, is from the hand of God, for without him, who can eat or find enjoyment?" (Eccles. 2:24-25).

A simple lifestyle is based on the assumptions that God will grant our basic needs and that the physical world is good as created by God. A Christian should not seek to accumulate more than he or she needs or can share wisely with the needy.

Like Koheleth, many narcissists have tried to achieve meaning and purpose in life through the accumulation of material goods, but eventually they experience meaninglessness. A simple, modest lifestyle comes closer to the kind of life envisioned by Jesus for members of the kingdom of God. Praying for our daily bread in the context of a simple life can help Christians avoid the danger of narcissism—whether it takes the form of *preoccupation* with the physical or unnecessary *denial* of the physical.

I Am the Bread of Life

The primary meaning of daily bread is physical nourishment. But Jesus' life and ministry clearly point to his concern with spiritual needs as well. Some argue that the Christian faith deals primarily or exclusively with the spiritual needs of humanity (the so-called "hot" gospel). Others argue that we should focus on the physical or secular needs first ("social" gospel). Ideally, both the spiritual and secular needs should be met by Christian ministry, a view that might be called a "whole" gospel.

Jesus probably faced this issue of the relation of physical and spiritual needs in his temptations. For example, when Satan tempted him to turn the stones into bread to satisfy his personal hunger, Jesus responded, "It is written: 'Man does not live on bread alone, but on every word that comes from the mouth of God' " (Matt. 4:4).

Jesus did feed the hungry with physical bread, but he also offered spiritual nourishment. In the "Cotton Patch" version of this story, Satan is identified as the Confuser.[8] Indeed, the temptation was for Jesus to confuse physical needs with spiritual needs. Jesus came to satisfy both kinds of needs, but the priority was on the spiritual needs of humanity. Physical bread alone would lead to spiritual death.

On two significant occasions Jesus tried to guide an audience from a narrow attention to the physical to a concern for their spiritual well-being. He did not reject a legitimate concern for the physical but noted the deeper spiritual needs. Talking with the Samaritan woman at Jacob's well, Jesus offered water that would quench her deepest thirst (John 4:10-15).

The feeding of the 5,000 is a second time Jesus focused on the relation of physical and spiritual nourishment. The crowd was so impressed with the miraculous bread that they followed Jesus, seeking more of the same. Jesus taught them about himself as the living bread. "I am the bread of life. He who comes to me will never go hungry, and he who believes in me will never be thirsty" (John 6:35).

The kind of nourishment you seek reflects the kind of life you value. "You are what you eat" is true both spiritually and physically. The recent concern in our culture about cholesterol, for example, points to our fear of physical death at an early age. When Jesus promised "life," he typically used the Greek word for a special quality of life (*zoe*), not the word for ordinary physical existence (*bios*). Eternal *zoe* meant a life lived in relation to Jesus, not merely the continuation of ordinary life indefinitely. He said he had come "that they may have life, and have it to the full" (John 10:10).

How long have you lived? Anthony Campolo distinguishes mere existence from true life.[9] We may have existed for a number of years, but real life means a meaningful relationship to Jesus. An abundant life is based on relationships, not mere ticks of a clock; it is "the life that is truly life" (1 Tim. 6:19).

Preoccupation with spiritual nourishment sometimes leads to the charge of otherworldliness. Christians can seem so heavenly minded that they are of no earthly good, as the old saying goes. Recognizing the danger of being too spiritual, the temptation is to swing to the other extreme and ignore or reject the spiritual needs of humanity. Reductionism is the denial of the spiritual dimension of life with the attitude of nothing-but-ism. Reductionism says that people are "nothing but" their physical makeup or psychological behavior.

This attitude was illustrated in an episode in the "B. C." comic strip. One man says, "There's a cloud that looks like the smoldering disquietude of man's collective inhumanity to man."

The second man counters, "Looks like a popcorn ball to me."

The first asks, "Must you make a molehill out of everything?"

A reductionist claims that Christians make the simple molehill into something complex. The Christian responds that the reductionist tries to oversimplify the truly complex realities of life. The total person is a concern of Jesus and should be a legitimate focus of Christian prayer. Indeed, Christian prayer should be *pneumopsychosomatic* in orientation.[10] In other words, a holistic view of human nature requires a holistic view of prayer.

Prayer as Thanksgiving in an Age of Self-Sufficiency

Do you have a hard time saying "Thank you"? Recently I was on a coffee break with some friends when I discovered I had little money with me. I took a lot of good natured kidding about my poverty, and one friend gave me money. The next day I taped a coin on a card with the Scripture reference Romans 13:8 and put it under my friend's office door. "Owe no one anything," Paul had told the Roman Christians (RSV). Although I originally meant my repayment and prooftexting as a practical joke, I also realized that I don't like to feel indebted or dependent on others.

This mood of self-sufficiency is common in our culture. So-called self-made people who have excelled in areas such as business or politics are often idolized. This rugged individualism makes it difficult for us to respond with gratitude to other people. Earlier in our history the Protestant work ethic encouraged hard work and self-reliance. Everyone was to be industrious and to pull their own load. A similar attitude marks the television commercials for a major financial firm. They make money the old fashioned way: they earn it.

Some passages do seem to encourage this industrious, self-reliant attitude. The writer of Proverbs, for example, told the Hebrews to imitate the industry of the ant in preparing for winter (Prov. 6:6-11). A similar note is struck in Paul's letters to the Thessalonians. Paul had worked at his trade, tentmaking, while he was with them and urged them to work hard as well (1 Thess. 2:9; 4:11; 5:14). Because of their obsession with the return of Christ, however, some had quit their jobs and were passively waiting for Jesus. Paul reminded them of his rule. "If a man will not work, he shall not eat" (2 Thess. 3:10). Or, as one scholar paraphrased it, "No loaf to the loafer!"[1]

This emphasis on hard work is noteworthy in a time when some people seem to be workaholics—who go beyond being industrious and are actually addicted to their work.[2] My concern here, however, is that the industrious person might not see any need to express thanks, either to God or to other people who have assisted. In the classic western movie *Shenandoah*, Jimmy Stewart leads his family in prayer before the meal. Although he is saying thanks to God, he continually reminds God how the family had worked so hard to cultivate the land, harvest the crop, and prepare the meal. Reference to God seems superfluous.

Biblical faith acknowledges the need for human effort without denying our interdependence with other people and our ultimate dependence on God. Paul did tell the Roman Christians to stay out of unnecessary debt but added in the same verse, "except the continuing debt to love one another" (Rom. 13:8).

Paul further noted that as Christians our lives are necessarily intertwined with the cause of Christ. "For none of us lives to himself alone and none of us dies to himself alone. If we live, we live to the Lord; and if we die, we die to the Lord. So, whether we live or die, we belong to the Lord" (Rom. 14:7-8).

In this chapter we will focus on two concerns related to gratitude in an age of self-sufficiency. First, we look at gratitude for the gift of Jesus. Paul found it easy to thank God for the gift of grace through Jesus (2 Cor. 9:15). Why should we be grateful for the gift of Jesus? How should we describe what God has done for us through Jesus? Second, we will consider those times when we do not feel like praying, when gratitude seems alien to our experience.

Thank You for Sending Your Son

The university where I teach has a fund-raising "phonathon." A few years ago I called an alumnus who happened to have a son in our school at the time. After I had explained what programs he could support through a contribution, the man declined, saying all the extra money he had was needed to continue supporting his son as he went through school.

I thanked him for his interest and said, "Thank you for sending your son."

As I hung up, another volunteer asked facetiously, "Who were you talking to, God?"

People laughed, but I later decided that thanking God for sending his Son, Jesus, was appropriate for a Christian.

Perhaps the most familiar verse in the Bible is John 3:16. "For God so loved the world that he gave his one and only Son, that whoever believes in him shall not perish but have eternal life." Central to that text is the emphasis on Jesus as the gift of God to humanity. If we perceive Jesus as God's gift to us, then our response should be gratitude. Jesus' disciples responded that way, but others either ignored him or rejected him.

Why should Christians give thanks for Jesus? Exactly what has he done for us? Theologians often divide the discussion of Jesus into two aspects, Christology and soteriology.[3] *Christology* deals with the identity of Jesus or the "person" of Christ. It normally includes examination of his deity, his humanity, and the unity of his person. *Soteriology* involves the "work" of Christ, or what he has done to make salvation available to us, including discussion of the various theories of the atonement.

Our discussion will focus on soteriology, or the work of Christ. What has Christ done for us? How we understand Jesus' work affects our gratitude for our salvation. Factors such as biblical study, personal experience, and our cultural setting have shaped how each of us perceives Jesus.[4] One way to discover what Jesus has done for us is to look for times he told us why he came. We have already seen that he described his task as the bringing of true, abundant life (John 10:10). After his encounter with Zacchaeus, Jesus said he "came to seek and to save what was lost" (Luke 19:10).

When James and John had requested places of prominence in the kingdom, Jesus replied that he came "to serve, and to give his life as a ransom for many" (Mark 10:45). When Jesus ate with tax collectors and sinners, the religious leaders complained. Jesus described his mission. "For I have not come to call the righteous, but sinners" (Matt. 9:13). On these occasions and others, Jesus used a variety of images to describe what he came to accomplish. For each of these tasks, the appropriate response would include gratitude.

Although all of Jesus' life and ministry is significant for Christians, our gratitude usually focuses on his death and resurrection. Again, a variety of New Testament word pictures or images were used to try to capture this central complex of events. Paul used three images as he introduced the topic of salvation in his letter to the Romans. Having just concluded that all people are sinners, he described the gift of Christ like this: Christians "are justified freely by his grace through the redemption that came by Christ Jesus. God presented him as a sacrifice of atonement, through faith in his blood" (Rom. 3:24-25).

First, Jesus justified us. For Paul, accused persons were justified when pardoned for crimes. The persons were really guilty, but the judge ruled that they would be treated as if they were innocent. Paul used a legal term in a nonlegalistic way since God did not give us what we deserved.

A friend of mine once autographed his book for me and included the line, "May you get everything you deserve." He knew that no one really wants what they deserve. If God dealt with us purely on the basis of justice, we would all be condemned for our sins. Instead, we are justified by God's grace.

Second, Jesus redeemed us. The basic meaning of the Greek word for redemption is liberation. Coming from the practice of slavery in the ancient world, redemption refers to the liberation of an enslaved person. Paul frequently noted the liberation theme in his discussion of salvation. Later in Romans, for example, he noted we are set free from slavery to sin (6:18-23).

Paul's emphasis on liberation echoes Jesus' own description of his ministry. At Nazareth, Jesus read Isaiah 61:1-2 as his sermon text. Included in his ministry would be proclaiming freedom for the captives and release to the oppressed (Luke 4:18-19). This message and ministry of liberation is so central to Jesus' life that one scholar entitled his book, *Jesus Means Freedom*.[5]

Third, Jesus was a "sacrifice of atonement" for our sins. The New International Version uses a phrase to translate one Greek word (*hilasterion*). The root meaning of the word could be translated "mercy seat," for it refers to the top of the ark of the covenant. The mercy seat was where the high priest sprinkled the blood of sacrificial animals on the Day of Atonement (Lev. 16:14-16). Paul here pointed to Jesus as the fulfillment of the Old Testament sacrificial system. Jesus is both the perfect High Priest and the perfect sacrificial victim.[6]

Why should we be grateful for Jesus? Paul's three images may not communicate as quickly to us as to a first-century reader, but through them we can catch a glimpse of Jesus' gift to us.

One Easter season the comic strip "B. C." reminded readers of the deeper meaning of the phrase "Thank God, it's Friday." The character reads the dictionary definition for "Good Friday": "The only Friday truly worthy of thanks to God."

In Christian tradition, Good Friday has been the nickname for the day Jesus was crucified. Although Jesus' death was agonizing, it was good in the sense that it made salvation available to us.

Perhaps we are so familiar with the story of Jesus' life, death, and resurrection that we are not really grateful for it. A few years ago a rereading of C. S. Lewis' children's book, *The Lion, the Witch and the Wardrobe* reminded me how powerful Christ's death would have been to the early Christians.[7] Aslan the lion represents Christ in this story. A boy had betrayed his brother and sisters. According to the law, he deserved to be killed by the wicked queen. But Aslan voluntarily took the boy's place and died for him. Lewis once said that all his books were evangelistic; certainly this children's story graphically retells the death and resurrection of Jesus.[8]

Historically, theologians have developed these various images and word pictures for Christ's work into theories of the atonement.[9] Although no one theory has drawn unanimous assent, all have tried to explain the significance of Christ's work for us. Our expressions of gratitude to God for sending his Son normally do not require our knowledge of the fine points of doctrinal history, but these images and theories can remind us of the reason for our gratitude—Jesus, the gift of God to humanity. Our salvation is a gift from God (Eph. 2:8-9).

I Don't Feel Like Praying

Do you always feel like praying? Or, to narrow the topic, do you always feel grateful to God? A traditional mealtime prayer says, "Oh, Lord, for what we are about to receive, make us truly thankful. Amen." In the "Beetle Bailey" comic strip, the chaplain prays that prayer, looks at his food again, and continues, "I guess I'm not getting through, am I?"

Does that traditional prayer really mean that sometimes God has to "make us" thankful? Isn't gratitude supposed to be spontaneous and natural?

The Christian life is often a series of peaks and valleys. We yearn to have a continual succession of mountaintop experiences, but life is punctuated with periods of mundane existence. In C. S. Lewis' classic, *The Screwtape Letters*, a senior devil gives advice to a junior devil about how to handle a human being. Screwtape tells Wormwood that the Christian life often follows the law of undulation. That is, "periods of emotional and bodily richness and liveliness will alternate with periods of numbness and poverty."[10] Such peaks and valleys are totally natural for humans, says Screwtape, but devils can take advantage of the trough periods for temptation.

Borrowing from Karl Rahner, Martin Marty developed the notion of two types of spirituality, wintry and summery.[11] A summery spirituality is more optimistic, upbeat, and positive. Marty insists, however, that the Christian faith allows for a wintry sort of piety in which the absence of the experience of God is acknowledged. Drawing especially from some of the Psalms, such as the laments, Marty sketches a spirituality for the low points of life. One value of Marty's study, like Lewis' law of undulation, is that it reminds us that life, even for Christians, is not always trouble-free.

When we as Christians fail to have this overall perspective on the pilgrimage of faith, we can have real difficulty with prayer as thanksgiving. Thanksgiving may be easier when we are on a spiritual mountaintop, but Paul urged us to "give thanks in all circumstances" (1 Thess. 5:18). Jennings notes,

> To give thanks *in* all things is not the same as giving thanks *for* all things. There exists in some of our churches an unnatural and un-holy piety that attributes to God all manner of evil and destruc-tion, and tells people that they ought to be thankful for that which is obviously destructive and *dis*-spiriting.[12]

I'm sure my daughter occasionally has a bad day, but she still thanks God for everything and everyone. If we forget the law of undulation, we can easily exaggerate how bad the bad days are. And we can unrealistically dream of an uninterrupted stream of mountaintop experiences.

Two scriptural mountaintop experiences remind us that peaks are often followed by return to the "real world," a world of ad-versity and service. When Elijah went to Mount Horeb to escape Jezebel, God spoke to him in the still small voice. God's instruc-tion to him was to return to Israel and carry on his ministry (1 Kings 19:15-18). He had retreated long enough on the moun-taintop. Now it was time for action. Jesus responded in a similar way when Peter wanted to linger on the mount of transfigura-tion. Jesus led the disciples down the mount to where a child needed to be healed (Mark 9:2-18).

Sometimes periods of discouragement seem so overwhelm-ing we lose our perspective. We forget that often there is some-thing positive about our experience we overlook while dwelling on the negative.

In the "Peanuts" comic strip Lucy once concluded, "My life is a drag. . . . I'm completely fed up. I've never felt so low in my life."

Linus urged Lucy to count her blessings, but she insisted that she had nothing to be thankful for.

Linus interrupted, "Well, for one thing, you have a little broth-er who loves you. . . ."

As Lucy began to cry and hug him, Linus added, "Every now and then I say the right thing."

Lucy had succumbed to the temptation to focus too much on the negative side of her life. She had forgotten about family members such as Linus.

Lucy's isolationism is typical of a narcissistic outlook on life and a forgetfulness of the normal ups and downs of life. For thankfulness to be an ongoing dimension to our prayer life, we need to break out of our preoccupation with our feelings or moods by recalling the law of undulation. Christians need to cultivate a realistic understanding of life. In chapter eleven we will return to the problem of suffering and examine the biblical bases for such a view of life.

Thankfulness can be a constant element in our prayer life when we recognize that gratitude is not merely a response to the typical vicissitudes of life. Imagine how you would respond if, for example, you were imprisoned but were innocent. The apostle Paul had such an experience for several years, yet he began each of the "prison letters" with a thanksgiving section (Eph. 1:3-23; Phil. 1:3-11; Col. 1:3-14; Philem. 4-7). In the last letter he wrote, Paul again could express thanks from prison (2 Tim. 1:3-7).

Perhaps the best insight into Paul's response to his imprisonment comes in his letter to Philippi. Despite being in jail, he says he is "content" (Phil. 4:11-12). How could he be content while unfairly imprisoned? The Greek word translated "content" was used by the ancient Stoics for self-sufficiency. They responded stoically to such situations by rationally suppressing their emotional response. Their approach to life stressed self-control and self-sufficiency. Although Paul used the same word, we realize from looking at the context in this passage that he is not promoting an individualistic self-sufficiency. Rather, he points to at least two factors in his contentment.

First, his contentment was not based on a rugged individualism. Even when his Philippian friends had not been able to show their concern for him in a tangible fashion, he knew that they had such a concern. When they were able to send gifts, he was grateful. The Greek root for the word translated "share" (Phil. 4:15) is also the basis for the word *koinonia*, frequently translated as fellowship, community, or partnership. Paul realized that he was not in this predicament alone. Physically isolated at times, he was content because of the concern of the Christians at Philippi.

Second, Paul was content because of his relationship to God. Paul's sufficiency was not a self-sufficiency but a God-sufficiency.[13] Paul says he "can do everything through him who gives me strength" (Phil. 4:13). The God in whom he trusts "will meet all your needs according to his glorious riches in Christ Jesus" (Phil. 4:19). Paul could express gratitude while in prison because of his relationship to other Christians and to God.

The tension many feel today is between a theology of gratitude, expressed by Paul's prison letters, and a theology of gratification, expressed by much of our popular culture. M. Scott Peck, a psychiatrist, was having difficulty determining why a woman procrastinated doing her work. Finally, he asked her if she liked cake. After a positive answer, he asked her how she ate a piece of cake. Her reply revealed her underlying approach to life. "I eat the frosting first, of course!"[14] Peck then tried to encourage her to adopt a view of life that included the value of delayed gratification.

Narcissists would easily identify with the woman's response. They want the best first, not last. Such an emphasis on gratification conflicts with a Christian approach to life. Seeking immediate gratification is more typical of a young child or narcissist than a person committed to a Christian value system. Like Paul, Christians strive to learn the secret of gratitude in all circumstances. Christian gratitude transcends the good days and the bad days of life because it is based on God-sufficiency rather than self-sufficiency.

9

Can You Shake Hands?

Has anyone ever confessed a sin to you? A few years ago I received a surprising letter from a former student. In his letter he confessed that he had cheated on the final exam in the last course he had taken with me. I'm not sure he was aware that my school's punishment for cheating is F for the course, but his conscience had been pricked and he felt he had to confess. If I now gave the F, he would lose the credit for the course. Since the course happened to be the last one he took for graduation, the university would have to recall his degree!

Sin, repentance, and forgiveness are major concerns of biblical faith. Jesus included them in the Lord's Prayer. He told his followers to pray, "Forgive us our debts, as we also have forgiven our debtors" (Matt. 6:12). Jesus is clearly calling for confession of sins by Christians and for Christians to be willing to forgive others. Indeed, this is the only petition in the Model Prayer that Jesus chose to develop further in that same context (see Matt. 6:14-15).

In this chapter we will spotlight the role of sin, confession, and forgiveness in Christian prayer. How have these concerns been influenced by the prevalence of narcissism? Generally, the influence of narcissism makes it harder for us to acknowledge our sin or to see sin's impact on those around us. In the first section we will clarify some aspects of a Christian view of sin. In the second section we turn to forgiveness, both divine and human. In the next chapter we will zero in on the difficulty of confessing sins in a world marked by narcissistic self-deception.

Is Your Mother a Better Person Than Hitler?

Sin has probably never been a popular topic of discussion, but some people believe there has been a decline of attention to sin in recent years. Karl Menninger's best-selling *Whatever Became of Sin?* focused attention on this and also stirred fresh discussion of sin in popular circles.[1]

Before Menninger's book revitalized the use of the term *sin,* one of my professors noted that people then were more disturbed at being labeled with psychological categories such as "neurotic" than being called "sinners." Sin was considered too old-fashioned to provide a useful model for analyzing the human predicament.

As a theologian, however, I am convinced that sin is an appropriate category for understanding the human condition. Other disciplines, such as the social sciences, literature, and philosophy provide helpful perspectives. But sin gives us the necessary depth and breadth of context to grasp our human predicament. In this section we will look at four aspects of the Christian view of sin.

Sin Is Sin?

How would you define sin? One approach is to focus on the key biblical terms that highlight the nature of sin. In the New Testament, for example, *hamartia,* or missing the mark, is a common word for sin. Related terms for sin include *adikia* (injustice), *anomia* (lawlessness), *parabasis* (transgression), *apostasia* (rebellion).

Our basic understanding of sin might be tested by an odd question. Is there any real difference between your mother and Hitler? Of course, there is a quantum leap, morally and spiritually, between my mother and Hitler. My mother is not perfect, but she certainly would never attempt the genocide of any group. Yet, one familiar aspect of the Christian view of sin is the aphorism, "Sin is sin." Not a meaningless statement or a tautology, this concept was usually coupled with the popular saying, "The ground at the foot of the cross is level." In other words, in the eyes of God we are all sinners. Shoplifting and bank robbery are both sins.

Quite likely the underlying concern in this "sin is sin" axiom is to stress that ultimately sin is a theological category rather than a moral category. Sin breaks our relationship with God. Sin may have consequences for our relationship with other people and even the physical world, but fundamentally sin affects our relation to God. When David confessed his adultery with Bathsheba, he said to God, "Against you, you only, have I sinned and done what is evil in your sight" (Ps. 51:4).

Although I hear "sin is sin" often in evangelical circles, I recognize also that we still tend to rank or prioritize certain sins. In everyday life we think of some sins as being worse than others. When *People* magazine asked its readers to rank 51 activities according to how guilty they would feel on committing them, the worst sin in their "sindex" was murder. The least sinful was "taping off TV or radio."[2] If "sin is sin" were the only way we looked at sin, such a ranking would be impossible.

Even if we grant that ultimately sin is a broken relation with God, we need to be concerned with our relation to other people. An egocentric person, such as Hitler must have been, might have the capacity to attract many followers and slaughter millions. Reinhold Niebuhr, for example, affirmed the equality of sin but added the notion of the inequality of guilt. He defined guilt as "the objective and historical consequences of sin."[3]

We can make a valid moral distinction between Hitler and our mothers in terms of the public consequences of sins. Hitler's sin, although equal to my mother's sin as a broken relation to God, caused tidal waves on the ocean of human history. My mother's sin, by contrast, made mere ripples on the same ocean. "Sin is sin" reminds us that sin is primarily a wrenching of our relation with God—but sins differ significantly in their impact on others, ourselves, and the created world.

Watching All the Girls Go By

A few years ago a woman wrote to "Dear Abby" about the difference between an evil thought and an evil action. "Somewhere in the Bible, it says that thinking lustful thoughts is as great a sin as actually committing the sin. So, if that is the case, why not go right ahead and commit the sin?"[4]

Probably the text the writer had in mind was Jesus' comment on adultery and lust in the Sermon on the Mount (Matt. 5:27-30). This comment was part of a series of comparisons between the Old Testament law and Jesus' interpretation of those laws. In these comparisons Jesus highlighted the importance of the attitude or thought.[5] Although Old Testament morality had some concern for motive, Jesus intensified that interest here.

Was the writer to "Dear Abby" correct in interpreting this passage to mean the thought was just as bad as the action? If so, go ahead and commit the deed! Scholars use the term *antinomianism* for this attitude.[6] Antinomianism literally means an opposition to the law (*nomos*), but it can refer to the attitude that we are above the law.

Antinomianism, or libertinism, is an excessive emphasis on freedom. If attitudes and actions are morally equal, or if sin is sin, then go right on with the deed. If lust is the same as adultery, why stop at lust? An old barbershop quartet song describes some men standing on the corner watching all the girls go by. It adds that you can't go to jail for what you're thinking. But can you commit a sin by thinking?

Surely Jesus is saying that the thought, like the deed, is sinful, but he is not necessarily suggesting that the thought is just as bad as the deed. For example, there seems to be a clear difference in public consequences between murdering someone and being angry with them (Matt. 5:21-22). Certainly the victims of character assassination and verbal abuse can sometimes wish they were dead, but in fact they can live and perhaps rebuild their lives.

One of Jesus' concerns in these comparisons of attitude and action may have been to help his audience see that all were sinners. Although the Bible frequently affirms that all have sinned, some stories stress that some people fail to see that they are sinners. The story of the adulterous woman, for example, reminds us that the accusers as well as the accused were sinners. The accusers knew she was a sinner, but Jesus confronted them with their own sin when he said that someone without sin could cast the first stone (John 8:7).

In Nathaniel Hawthorne's classic novel, *The Scarlet Letter*, the adulterous woman wore a red "A" on her clothing as a badge of dishonor for her sin. Ranking some sins as more serious than others can be dangerous, because we often think other people commit the major sins, while our sins are minor. To be more consistent and less judgmental, we might all wear a letter of the alphabet to symbolize our sins. We could have "L" for liars, "R" for racists, "P" for plagiarists, and so on. Such a practice is unnecessary as long as we have a healthy appreciation for the universality of sin, acknowledging that sin can be internal as well as external, private as well as public.

A Theology for Couch Potatoes

Do you ever feel guilty for *not* doing something? Some Christians distinguish between sins of *commission* and sins of *omission*. A sin of commission is a bad deed that you do. You commit murder, theft, adultery, or lying. A sin of omission is described briefly in James 4:17. "Anyone, then, who knows the good he ought to do and doesn't do it, sins." Your commitment to certain priorities may result in a lack of time for worthier goals.

Significantly, James' description of the sin of omission follows his description of people who are planning to travel to certain cities and making money (James 4:13). Planning for the future seems harmless, yet James warns that their plans reflect a lack of awareness about what the future might bring. "What is your life?" (James 4:14). Life is a mist that soon disappears like the early morning fog.

These business people apparently have planned their lives in total disregard of God. Although they might not be especially selfish, they at least need to consider God's will in their decision-making. "If it is the Lord's will, we will live and do this or that" should be their motto (James 4:15). Tennessee Ernie Ford's motto on his old television program echoes this sentiment. He would be back on the air the next week "if the good Lord's willin' and the creek don't rise!"

The sin of omission characterizes couch potatoes. Couch potatoes are people who spend inordinate amounts of time watching television. They vegetate as they become increasingly passive. Life for them is a spectator sport. Jesus' parable of the good Samaritan illustrates a theology for couch potatoes (Luke 10:25-37). The robbers were guilty of the sin of commission as they robbed and beat the victim. But the priest and the Levite were guilty of the sin of omission because they failed to do the good deed they should have.

The sin of omission is closely related to the sin of doing what comes naturally. Some people feel no need to control or discipline themselves. They simply do what seems natural. Reinhold Niebuhr termed this type of sin "sensuality."[7] Although he believed that pride or arrogance was the fundamental form of human sin, he noted that sensuality was also common.

Both pride and sensuality arise from our being free and finite as creatures of God. Pride reflects the choice to place self rather than God at the center of existence. Proud persons deny their finitude and accent only their freedom. Sensual persons, on the other hand, deny their freedom and accent their finitude. Instead of trying to control their natural impulses, they do whatever they feel like doing. Sensuality, like pride, is a form of self-love.

Niebuhr apparently chose sensuality as the label for this type of self-love because it often is a distortion of some physical desire such as sex. Sex itself is certainly not sinful, but its drives make us especially vulnerable to sin. Besides physical desires, sensuality might express itself through conformity to peer pressure. Rather than critically examining what your social group proposes to do, you go with the flow.

When Erich Fromm asked why Hitler's totalitarianism was so attractive, he found a clue in the human inclination to escape from freedom because freedom is so frightening. Rather than trying to exercise freedom responsibly, many people found it easier to let someone else make their decisions for them.[8]

Niebuhr and others may be correct in seeing pride as the fundamental form of sin, but in this century sensuality has been especially prominent. If Hitler can represent the worst form of egotism or arrogance, then Adolf Eichmann can represent sensuality or apathy. Eichmann helped Hitler attempt genocide by "doing what he was told, keeping his nose clean, and seeing to it that the trains ran on time."[9] Sensuality can be a form of narcissism because the couch potato is concerned with self-preservation. Although Eichmann may not have been an egotist like Hitler, he watched out for himself rather than protest genocide.

Achan's Kin

So far we have seen that sin is sin; that even if guilt might not be equal, sin can be an attitude as well as an action; and that sin can be accomplished by omission as well as commission. One other issue deserves brief attention. Is sin always the act of an individual? Is sin ever collective?

A intriguing Old Testament story about sin is Achan's theft of some valuable items in the conquest of Jericho. Although Joshua and the Hebrews were under strict orders not to take any spoils of war as they invaded Canaan, Achan disobeyed. When Achan's sin was made public, he and his family were killed for breaking the rules of holy war (Josh. 7:24-26).

Achan's family might have been willing accomplices in crime. But the execution of the whole family seems harsh to contemporary Christians. Why not just kill the guilty person?

One frustrating aspect of Achan's story is the way it clashes with our individualism. I noticed this when I assigned group projects in one of my classes. Four or five students would work together and report their findings to the whole class. Since all I could observe was the final report to the class, not the work of the individuals, I gave the same grade to each member of the group. Almost invariably someone in the group would complain. "All of us except Tim worked really hard, yet you gave us all a B. That's not fair. We deserved A's."

Although individual responsibility is a major theme in Scripture, the Bible does stress our interdependence as well. As our culture tends to stress individualism at the expense of collective responsibility, so evangelical Christians sometimes over-emphasize individual sins. For a while evangelical Christians shied away from emphasis on sin being incarnate in systems or institutions because it might sound like a revival of the social gospel of the turn of the last century. Liberation theologians have increasingly reminded other Christians that we need to de-privatize sin. Groups can be sinful. Racism, sexism, and other ideologies often represent institutional forms of sin.[10]

Growing up in a racist environment and time period, I never felt that I was really a racist. A black theologian might tell me, however, that I was indirectly involved in a racist society. Since I rarely spoke out against the racism that pervaded my culture, I was guilty of racism. By doing nothing, I allowed an evil institution to go unchallenged.

Father, Forgive Them

Although we only glanced at a few aspects of the Christian understanding of sin, we began to see that sin is a legitimate way to diagnose the human predicament. An obvious question, however, is, "If we are all sinners, is our situation hopeless?" Sometimes we so stress the bad news of the depth of human sin that we neglect the good news of God's grace and forgiveness.

Having sketched key features of a Christian doctrine of sin, we need to address the doctrine of forgiveness. In this section we will look at two aspects of forgiveness—God's forgiveness of our sins and our forgiveness of other human beings. The link between these dimensions is clear in the Lord's Prayer (Matt. 6:12).

Forgive Us Our Debts

Have you ever felt you were so bad that you were beyond help? Several times in my life I've tried some new activity and decided I could never master it. Perhaps I did not have the patience or discipline to learn the new skill, but I really thought I was so bad that I might as well give up. I tried ice skating once. And once was enough! I was mediocre at best at roller skating and terrible at ice skating.

Some people believe that because they have sinned God has given up on them. The young man who wrote me to confess his cheating quoted part of Jeremiah 17:9. "The heart is deceitful above all things. . . . Who can understand it?" I was glad he left out, perhaps on purpose, the phrase "and beyond cure." Although he felt terrible about cheating on my test, he had confessed his sin to God and now was writing me.

Some people might identify more with the comic strip character Nancy. Coming into her house after playing in her yard, she noticed she had left a trail of muddy footprints. She tried to clean the floor, but, because she forgot to take off her muddy shoes, new tracks appeared. She concluded, "I'm not sure if this is just housework, or some sort of sobering metaphor for life. . . ."

How does God react to our sin? For a long time I operated with a subconscious view of God as being like an elementary school teacher during a spelling bee. I could spell reasonably well, but I knew that if I made a mistake, I was out of the competition. There were no second chances in our school's spelling bees. Somehow I had decided that if I sinned, God would reject me. I heard preachers say that God hated the sin and loved the sinner, but at the existential level I thought God probably disliked both the sin and the sinner.

The Bible is clear that sin displeases God. One popular understanding of divine displeasure is that God gets "mad" when we sin. For some, scriptural references to the wrath of God reinforce this one-sided view of God's disfavor, but if we try to ignore or rationalize this concept, we might move close to viewing God as a permissive grandparent. God's wrath is not the same as when you or I get mad, but God does dislike our rebellion.

Another biblical image for divine disfavor is God's sadness at our sin. Like a parent who sees a child mess up, God is disappointed at our sin. Hosea, for example, spoke of God responding in anguish rather than the heat of anger at the rebellious Hebrews (Hosea 11:1-3, 8-9). When we sin, we not only break God's laws, we break God's heart. The Hebrew prophets often noted God's grief over the Hebrews' failure to honor their covenant commitment to Yahweh.[11]

Alongside of the frequent biblical emphasis on divine displeasure at sin is a stress on God's willingness to forgive and be reconciled to God's people. For example, the psalmist noted that he does not treat us as our sins deserve or repay us according to our iniquities. For as high as the heavens are above the earth, so great is his love for those who fear him (Ps. 103:10).

Although Paul often noted our sinful condition, he also emphasized that we live in a pre-forgiven world. "But God demonstrates his own love for us in this: While we were still sinners, Christ died for us" (Rom. 5:8). God does not wait for us to cower and grovel, saying, "I'll think about forgiving you when I'm convinced you've crawled enough!" Instead, God is predisposed to forgive us.

Throughout his ministry Jesus taught and modeled the forgiveness of God. He often associated with the sinners and outcasts of society. What his enemies considered a disgrace, he considered an act of grace.[12] When he was on the cross, he prayed, "Father, forgive them, for they do not know what they are doing" (Luke 23:34). Because of his intimate relation with the Father, Jesus knew that God was a forgiving God.

Forgive Our Debtors

Do you find it easy to forgive someone who has wronged you? Lewis Smedes summarizes the encounter of a French journalist and a German war criminal from Michael Christopher's play, *The Black Angel*.[13] The Frenchman's family had been killed in World War II, and he had pursued the German. Having alerted the villagers of the presence of this war criminal in a nearby cabin, the journalist went to confront the criminal.

After a long conversation, the journalist began to see the criminal as a feeble human being. He offered to lead the criminal to safety before the villagers came to kill him. The criminal agreed to flee on one condition—the journalist must forgive the criminal. The journalist refused, and the criminal died.

Many of us have a hard time making the transition from being forgiven by God to forgiving other people. Jesus' parable of the unmerciful servant illustrates how the forgiven man failed to be forgiving (Matt. 18:21-35). Jesus told the parable in response to Peter's question about how many times we should forgive someone who sins against us. Having had a very large debt canceled, the servant refused to cancel the much smaller debt of another man.

In one comic strip two people notice the bulletin board announcing Sunday's sermon topic as "Forgive Human Eror." One man notes, "There are two R's in error." The other man stalks off saying, "That stupid janitor!"

When we are wronged by another person, we have at least three possible responses. First, we might seethe with *resentment*. We might never do or say anything to the person who offended us, but inwardly we harbor ill will. Bottling up that kind of negative feeling is hazardous to our emotional and spiritual health. Resentment can eventually poison our relations with other people, even when they are not the objects of the resentment.

Second, we could seek to retaliate or get *revenge*. The old saying, "Don't get mad, get even," makes sense to a lot of people. Television shows and motion pictures glamorize a vindictive attitude. Many of the "heroes" of these shows and movies practice a violent, eye for an eye approach to problem-solving. Scripture instructs believers to let God take care of revenge (e.g., Deut. 32:35; Prov. 20:22; 25:21-22; 1 Pet. 3:3-12).

A problem with individual retaliation is that we place ourselves in the place of God. If we knew everything like God does, we would know a situation well enough to determine how justice should prevail. Since we are finite, sinful beings, we tend to be judgmental. We notice the others' flaws but fail to recognize our own (Matt. 7:1-5). Jesus clearly taught an attitude of nonretaliation in the Sermon on the Mount. While the Old Testament law limited revenge to an eye for an eye, Jesus criticized the urge to get even (Matt. 5:38-42).

Either resentment or retaliation might characterize a self-centered person. Narcissists have thin skins and are easily offended. Their rights or privileges are easily infringed. They claim to want justice when self-interest is the primary motivation. Their sense of rivalry with others oversensitizes them to insult.

The third and best response to being wronged is *reconciliation*. Jesus sketched a process for reconciliation that begins with a private conference (Matt. 18:15-20). If reconciliation does not occur here, then two or three consult with the offending person. Eventually, if the offending person is unrepentant, the issue is brought to the whole congregation. Throughout the process the goal is reconciliation, not revenge. The church is to be gracious and forgiving to the repentant sinner.

When children have fights, parents often try to mediate. A common rule in my childhood was to symbolize the reconciliation by having the combatants shake hands. The hand shake became a sign of unity rather than a mere social custom.

After surviving a German concentration camp, Corrie Ten Boom began a ministry of writing and speaking about her experiences. One night in Munich she recognized a man in the crowd as a German soldier from the concentration camp. Now a Christian also, he asked her to forgive him. At first Corrie Ten Boom had difficulty forgiving him, but after some hesitation she shook his hand. Because she had been forgiven by God, she could forgive others.[14]

10

Prayer as Confession in an Age of Self-Deception

Have you confessed any sins lately? If so, what prompted the confession? When I received that letter (chapter nine) from the student admitting cheating on my exam, I was curious about what had happened after a couple of years to trigger the letter.

He wrote that he had been doing a spiritual inventory, and God "pricked my heart." Perhaps his private prayer included such a recalling of his past life. A few months ago a different student called me at home to confess a similar sin. He volunteered that he had come to an honest awareness of his sin and the need to talk to me while he was in a public worship service.

For many denominations public worship includes a time for confession of sin.[1] Participants do not normally mention specific sins, but at least the community of faith acknowledges the presence of sin in their lives. Sometimes a religious leader discusses sin in such a direct way that we cannot fail to see our sins. One of my students wore a T-shirt with the message "Turn or Burn!" but most religious leaders are less confrontational.

When a comic strip figure asks the preacher why he's been on "lover's lane," the minister replies, "Writing Sunday's sermon."

The worried parishioner asks, "Are you going to give names?"

Sometimes the Hebrew prophets were very direct in condemning sins and sinners, even giving names. When Saul impatiently offered a sacrifice before Samuel arrived, Samuel minced no words in pronouncing God's judgment. Saul would lose his role as king! (1 Sam. 13:8-14).

God sometimes reminds us of our sins in more subtle ways. One very effective way we are confronted with our sin is through stories. After David committed adultery with Bathsheba, for example, the prophet Nathan told David a story. A rich man had taken a poor man's only lamb in order to prepare a meal for a guest. When David expressed a deep sense of outrage at this injustice, Nathan added, "You are the man!" (2 Sam. 12:7). David then confessed his sin (2 Sam. 12:13; Ps. 51).

Clarence Jordan described Nathan's parable as a literary Trojan horse.[2] Like the large, hollow wooden horse left for the citizens of Troy, the story seemed simple and innocuous at first, but it led to David realizing his sin in a fresh way.

Has God ever used a story to sneak up on you? A friend of mine, knowing my appreciation for Dr. Seuss' children's stories, gave me *The Butter Battle Book*. The story revolves around the conflict between the Yooks and the Zooks. The conflict escalates until both sides have developed sophisticated armaments.

The end of the book is open-ended. Both sides have new weapons, but will they use them? The last page of the book frustrated me and surprised me. I expect children's books to have neat endings such as "and they lived happily ever after." Obviously Dr. Seuss was writing a modern parable about the nuclear arms race, implying that we all can influence how the story ends.

I had a similar experience near the end of the movie, *The Mission*. Based on the ministry of some Roman Catholic missionaries to South American Indians during a political power struggle, the movie closes with two politicians discussing the recent slaughter of several missionaries and Indians at one mission.

Apparently justifying the necessity for the slaughter, one man says, "The world is thus."

The other man responds, "No, we have made the world thus."

The screenwriter apparently wanted to confront the viewers with our uncritical acceptance of the status quo.

In this chapter we will examine confession as a crucial element in Christian prayer. Although the Bible indicates that we need to confess our sins to other people (James 5:16) and seek to be reconciled to those we have wronged, our focus here will be on confession to God.

I'm OK, You're OK?

A popular stereotype of Christianity is that it is negative and pessimistic about human nature. Since mainstream Christianity talks about original sin, the universality of sin, and total depravity, some people have concluded that any discussion of self-worth, self-respect, or self-esteem is alien to the Christian thought. The popularity of books such as *I'm OK, You're OK* reflects a widespread felt need for a higher self-concept.[3]

In this section we will explore the relation of confession of sins to the narcissistic dimension of our culture. Can we have a realistic view of our sinfulness without denying being creatures of God, made in God's image and likeness? Can we affirm a legitimate self-worth without becoming narcissistic?

The current interest in narcissism reflects at least two objections to a Christian doctrine of sin—Christianity is life-denying and Christians are hypocrites. On examination I believe both objections will turn out to be half-truths or misconceptions. A more balanced, complete understanding of sin avoids both problems.

First, a narcissist might object that Christians have labeled anything enjoyable as wicked. Christianity is totally legalistic and negative. According to this caricature, "If it feels good, it's bad." Underlying this depiction of Christian faith is the dualism that has often shadowed Christianity. Some Christians have taken physical pleasure to be sinful and developed an elaborate set of prohibitions on pleasure. The narcissist may follow up on this stereotype by suggesting, "If it feels good, it's good."

Some Christians have left themselves open to this misunderstanding by their descriptions of *flesh* and *spirit* in Paul's theology. Paul probably used these two categories for two value systems rather than two totally distinct parts of human nature. Living in the flesh meant anything that opposed God. Living in the spirit corresponded to a Christian value system.

In Galatians Paul contrasted these two ways of life (Gal. 5:19-23). The works of the flesh include physical actions as well as attitudes such as envy and selfishness. The fruit of the Spirit includes self-control, probably of the body as well as the emotions (see 1 Cor. 7:9; 9:25).

Physical desires can lead to sin, as James noted in his description of this sequence: desire, sin, death (James 1:14-15). The desire itself is not necessarily sinful. An old definition of sin is that sin is the illegitimate expression of a legitimate desire. Because our physical desires can be intense, we often notice them. But the physical desire is not the sin. Paul warned that the flesh can be an opportunity for sin (Gal. 5:13, RSV). The word translated "opportunity" is like a bridgehead in a battle and can refer to a vulnerability.[4]

The mistaken perception of Christianity as negative and life-denying created a context in which affirmation of self-worth seemed mutually exclusive with the Christian faith. Perhaps a more serious problem is the second concern of narcissists, that Christians are often hypocritical. There is an element of truth here, for Christians do fail to live up to the standards of Christ.

The underlying issue here is honesty in self-assessment. Many people have trouble in being honest with themselves about their problems. When they deceive themselves, then they try to be deceptive with other people and with God. In the now famous Pogo comic strip, Pogo said, "We have met the enemy and he is us."

Rather than accusing others of inconsistency, we must be honest with ourselves. The Reverend Will B. Dunn in the "Kudzu" comic strip once prayed, "Lord, smite mine enemies. . . . Smite 'em! Smite mine own worst enemy!" After the preacher is struck by lightning, he continues, "Let me rephrase that."

Self-deceit or self-deception is probably one of the most subtle effects of sin on our lives. We want to say we're okay rather than admit our sins to ourselves, to others, or to God. One reason we avoid this kind of disclosure is our fear of rejection. Admitting our failures to others will make us look weak, and we fear being vulnerable. Also we fear confessing to God because God might reject us as well.

In the first century the apostle John was concerned that some were practicing this kind of self-deception. He criticized those who claimed they were above sin, for those people deceived themselves (1 John 1:8-10). If we confess our sins, John insists, Jesus will forgive us and cleanse us from those sins. John later noted that the ideal is for Christians to be totally free from the power of sin (1 John 3:6-9). John was reacting against some who claimed sinless perfection and were arrogant and unloving towards others in the church.

Jesus encountered a similar self-deception among the religious leaders. When Jesus healed a blind man, these leaders complained that he had done the miracle on a Sabbath. The blind man became a believer in Jesus as well as receiving his physical sight. The leaders, who could see physically, had no insight into Jesus. They were truly blind (John 9:40). They were self-deceived about their true spiritual status.

A comprehensive, balanced understanding of sin would avoid the two objections just reviewed. Sin is not limited to physical actions. And self-deception affects the narcissist as well as the hypocrite. Saying "I'm okay" might reflect an evasion of sin.

In one cartoon a haggard man carrying a briefcase mumbles, "I'm number one. I'm number one. I'm number one. I'm. . . ." If he were honest with himself, he would acknowledge his true situation. Because of our sin, we are not okay. Because of the availability of God's grace, however, we can be okay.

Paul Tillich noted, "We cannot transform our lives, unless we allow them to be transformed by that stroke of grace. . . . *Simply accept the fact that you are accepted* [emphasis added]."[5] God accepts us as we are and makes the necessary transformation. The old Christian song, "Just as I Am," reminds us God accepts us just as we are, then enables us to become what we should be.

Truth or Consequences

The confession of sin in prayer is the connecting link between sin and salvation. Sincere confession taps the forgiveness of God and releases us from the bondage to sin. In this section we will focus on two topics related to confession as a type of Christian prayer. First, confession includes an honest acceptance of personal responsibility for our actions. Second, we will look at some of the consequences of confession.

First, authentic confession involves a candid acknowledgment of personal responsibility. "Who's responsible?" is a valid question in many of life's experiences. A few years ago I received a letter that began, "It's all my fault." Although I wasn't sure the writer was totally at fault, I did appreciate his candor and willingness to accept the blame for the situation. In one episode of the television series "M*A*S*H," Hawkeye Pierce was so frustrated at the Korean War that he sent a message to the president, simply asking, "Who's responsible?"

Although self-centered people take credit for a project that succeeds, they evade blame for failure. For example, Aaron had made a golden calf for the Hebrews to worship, but when Moses returned and confronted him, Aaron tried to pass the buck. He claimed he simply threw the gold into the fire, "and out came this calf!" (Exod. 32:24). Aaron was trying to save himself by avoiding the blame for the idolatry.

A more responsible attitude occurs in the ads for a brand of men's underwear. "Inspector 12" insists that she is responsible for the dependability of that clothing. Right or wrong, she'll take the responsibility.

A genuine sense of responsibility entails knowing *for what* you are responsible and *to whom* you are responsible. Both of these issues appear in one of the classic texts on responsibility, Ezekiel 18. The Hebrews were blaming their captivity in Babylon on the sins of their ancestors, citing a popular saying, "The fathers eat sour grapes, and the children's teeth are set on edge" (Ezek. 18:2). God told them to stop using the saying. The responsibility for their situation was theirs. By using three generations of a family tree, Ezekiel demonstrated the principle of individual responsibility (Ezek. 18:5-18).

If we confess our sins, our lives can be changed by God. When John the Baptist preached a message of repentance, some in his audience got specific directions about the consequences of repentance. People with extra clothing and food would share, tax collectors would collect only the required amount of money, and soldiers would stop extorting money and falsely accusing people (Luke 3:10-14). Repentance would produce a noticeable change in their lives. When Jesus ate dinner with Zacchaeus, the tax collector's life was changed. We do not know what Jesus said to Zacchaeus over dinner, but the result was Zacchaeus' offer to return money to his victims (Luke 19:8).

Confession of sin, linked to a commitment to Christ, has eternal and temporal consequences. A Christian prays that God's will be done, while the narcissist insists on doing what he or she selfishly wants to do. Sometimes confession of sin has dramatic temporal results. Improved family relations and better performance at work might accompany a candid confession of sin.

The eternal consequences of confession involve our relation to God. The Christian experiences salvation, and the person committed only to self suffers the consequences of that decision, traditionally known as the wrath of God. The best description of God's wrath in the New Testament comes in Paul's discussion of God's reaction to the ingratitude of the godless and wicked. They refused to give thanks to God for his revelation in the physical world and turned to idolatry (Rom. 1:21-23). Three times Paul described the consequent wrath of God operating when God gave them over to the decisions they had made (Rom. 1:24, 26, 28).

This description of the wrath of God does not fit the popular stereotype of the fire and brimstone. Instead of "zapping" us for our rebellion, God allows us to self-destruct.[6] Selfish people place themselves where God should be and will suffer the consequences of that decision.

In his short novel, *The Great Divorce*, C. S. Lewis described the journey of a bus load of people to the outskirts of heaven. Each passenger then faced the decision whether or not to go on to heaven. At one point the discussion focused on why some go to heaven and others do not. One character noted, "There are only two kinds of people in the end: those who say to God, 'Thy will be done,' and those to whom God says, in the end, 'Thy will be done.' And all in Hell choose it."[7] Confessional prayer is one of the key places in life where we can voice our decision about whose "will" we choose to follow, ours or God's.

11

Real Life, Real Answers

What is the secret of life? Everyone from gurus to philosophers to comic strip characters offers us secrets for living happy, successful lives. When Charlie Brown asks Lucy about the secret of life, Lucy's crisp answer is "elbow pads." She explains that elbow pads would help people avoid pain when they bump into desk corners and doors. Most of us want a more profound answer than elbow pads, but Lucy does recognize that many of us desire a life free of pain.

In the Lord's Prayer, Jesus taught his followers to pray, "And lead us not into temptation, but deliver us from the evil one" (Matt. 6:13). In this chapter we will spotlight a Christian perspective on the difficulties of life.

An old Celtic prayer reminds us of this concern. "From ghoulies and ghosties and long-legged beasties and things that go bump in the night . . . deliver us." Although such a prayer might sound superstitious to many contemporary people, the underlying concern is a perennial one—desire for deliverance from trouble. In the first section we will look at the topic of temptation to sin. In the second section we turn to the topic of evil and suffering. The next chapter focuses on lament as the kind of prayer typical when life seems out of our control.

Yield!

A few years ago, I noticed a new billboard—a large picture of french fries dominated the picture with the word "Yield!" at the top. Near the bottom was the name of a fast-food restaurant at the next exit on the interstate highway. I felt no inclination to stop, but I was intrigued by the strategy behind the billboard's message. Perhaps the restaurant wanted to create an appetite for french fries as much as satisfy a prior felt need. Just by portraying the fries so vividly, the restaurant might tempt the ordinary motorist. The fries would be the temptation, and one would, predictably, yield.

When Jesus told his disciples to pray for God not to lead them into temptation, he used a word that could be translated "temptation" or "test" (NEB, JB), or "hard testing" (TEV). *Temptation* has the negative connotation of trying to get someone to do evil, to sin.

Testing, however, means that someone's loyalty is being determined. The point of testing is to show the depth of conviction or loyalty to a value or belief. Ideally the person being tested will do well. James reminded his readers that God does not tempt us to do evil (James 1:13); God does, however, test God's people (Abraham, Job). In this part of the chapter, however, our focus will be on the topic of temptation. Testing as one of the purposes of suffering will reappear in the next section.

What is the source of your temptation? We all face temptation to sin, but the source of temptation may vary. Four possibilities deserve consideration. First, perhaps *God* is the source of temptation. As we noted above, James insisted that God is not a source of temptation. Instead, God is the source of good, not evil (James 1:17). Since God is Creator and Lord of the universe, however, God created the possibility of sin and evil. A deterministic view of God might require that God be the direct cause of evil and sin, but many Christians believe God allows sin to occur without directly causing it.

The second source of temptation is *ourselves*. After rejecting

God as the origin of temptation, James suggested inward desire as the source (James 1:14-15). Desires can be good, but sin occurs when they are expressed inappropriately. Hunger, for example, is a legitimate desire, but gluttony is a sinful expression of that desire. Paul criticized the libertines at Corinth for not controlling their desires. These libertines felt that they could eat whatever they wanted and have sex with anyone (1 Cor. 6:12-16). Paul responded by emphasizing that we can honor God with our bodies (1 Cor. 6:19-20).

A third source of temptation is *other people*. Friends, family, and associates might offer a suggestion about an attitude or activity contrary to God's standards. Paul, for example, warned, "Bad company corrupts good character" (1 Cor. 15:33). Psalm 1 compliments the righteous man because he avoided associating with the wicked (Ps. 1:1).

Christians cannot isolate themselves from other people, but they need to be aware of the dangerous consequences of peer pressure. Our friends and family members might tempt us to sin directly through a suggestion to do something wrong, or they might tempt us by distracting us from doing the right thing through involvement with some trivial matter.

A fourth source of temptation is the *devil*. Two of the most famous temptation stories in Scripture highlight the role of Satan. Although not mentioned by name in the story of Adam and Eve, the serpent represents the role Satan plays in the temptation of those two (Rev. 12:9). Satan's role is explicitly mentioned in the temptations of Jesus (Matt. 4:1-11).

Satan does tempt us, but a danger is using Satan as an alibi for our sins. "The devil made me do it!" was used by a popular comedian a few years ago as the excuse for all kinds of behavior. Concerning devils C. S. Lewis noted two dangers—not believing in them and being excessively interested in them.[1] We can acknowledge the significant role of Satan in temptation without an inordinate fear or preoccupation with him.

Related to Satan are New Testament references to the "powers." In Ephesians, for example, Paul warns of the spiritual warfare Christians must wage with the powers (Eph. 6:12). Traditionally, many Christians have seen these powers as supernatural beings such as demons or devils. Frank Peretti's novel about spiritual warfare, *This Present Darkness*, seems to epitomize this traditional stance.[2]

Some contemporary Christians complement this view by stressing that these powers can become incarnate in evil political and social institutions.[3] Richard Foster, for instance, identifies seven contemporary "powers" that need to be opposed by Christians: mammon, sex, religious legalism, technology, narcissism, militarism, and absolute skepticism.[4]

Since we face temptation from several sources, our prayers about temptation need to deal honestly with our weaknesses and vulnerable points. Three concrete examples of temptation might help our thinking. In *The Lion, the Witch and the Wardrobe* Edmund betrays his brother and two sisters for some candy, Turkish Delight. He loves the candy so much that he becomes a traitor.[5]

In the movie, *The Seduction of Joe Tynan*, a political leader is tempted by power. He neglects his family to gain political prestige and the chance to run for president. In Psalm 73 the writer expressed his jealousy of other people. The prosperity of the wicked troubled him, and he began to wonder why he had worked so hard at being good. The common thread through these three brief illustrations is the concern for self or narcissism. The pursuit of physical pleasure via Turkish Delight, political power, and prosperity all derive from obsession with self.

Being tempted does not necessarily lead to sin. Jesus was tempted but did not sin (Heb. 4:15). As humans we do sin, but we find many ways to rationalize our behavior.

Two cartoons show the same pig indulging in a sin. On one cartoon the caption reads, "Augustinian pig sinning because of his fallen nature." The other caption reads, "Pelagian pig sinning just because he wants to."[6]

Although the early church theologians Augustine and Pelagius debated the origin of sin, most Christians agree that we should pray for help with temptation. When Jesus' disciples had difficulty waiting while he prayed in the garden of Gethsemane, he noted, "Watch and pray so that you will not fall into temptation" (Mark 14:38). Acknowledging the temptation in prayer is a good starting point in our struggle with the temptation. Through prayer we put also ourselves in touch with the power of God in overcoming the temptation.

No Pain, No Gain?

Television commercials give us mixed signals about life's difficulties. On one hand, ads for physical fitness suggest, "No pain, no gain." On the other hand, an ad for a pain-reliever shows busy people saying, "I don't have time for the pain."

When Jesus told us to pray "deliver us from evil" he raised the issue of evil and suffering. The word translated "evil" could mean "evil one" and refer to Satan. Either as evil or evil *one*, the major concern is with the aspects of life that trouble us. Evil might be defined as anyone or anything that disrupts the harmony and unity of God's creation. Most of us consider something evil if it brings discomfort or dis-ease to us personally.

If we have a tendency toward narcissism, it probably surfaces when we encounter pain or suffering. A sharp physical pain, for example, causes us to be preoccupied with ourselves and oblivious to others. In her discussion of the three stages of suffering, Soelle noted that the first stage creates a sense of isolation and a turning in on oneself.[7] In the second stage we express our suffering through laments and often pray prayers with utopian dreams. In the third stage, we sense our solidarity with others.

In this section we will focus on a Christian perspective on suffering. We will look briefly at the possible causes of our suffering, then turn to the possible consequences of that suffering.[8]

Who Made This Mess?

The reality of suffering does not seem subject to much debate in Christian circles. Although some religions and philosophies argue that evil and suffering are illusory, Christianity holds to an "unflinching realism" about the presence of evil in human history.[9] What causes the suffering is open to more discussion. Is it God's fault or ours?

"Ultimately God is responsible for human suffering." When I said that to a Bible study group recently, one of my friends became visibly disturbed. He told me after the session that he could not accept that statement because he saw human suffering resulting primarily from human sin and errors. My response was to try to underscore the word "ultimately." God is not necessarily the direct cause of suffering, but God did create the kind of world in which Hitler, tornadoes, and leukemia are possibilities.

The two extremes I was trying to avoid were dualism and determinism. In *determinism* divine omnipotence has been transformed into divine omnicausality. We can say, "God can do anything" (omnipotence), without saying, "God has done everything" (omnicausality).

God is the ultimate cause of whatever happens because God created the context in which bad things can happen. *Dualism*, on the other hand, makes evil an eternal principle or personality alongside the good God. Dualists protect the good God from any responsibility for evil by assuming there is an evil being responsible for all the evil events of life.

My friend was properly wary of divine determinism, but I also wanted him to avoid the opposite danger of dualism. A popular hymn, "Like a River Glorious," suggests that "Ev'ry joy or trial Falleth from above."[10] The hymn writer is not necessarily a determinist for tracing all of life to God as the ultimate source.

Since God allows some elbow room in the universe, some of the responsibility for human suffering is ours. Human sin, the misuse of human freedom, is one cause of suffering. God created us with finite freedom, and if we mess up we suffer consequences.

Is suffering, then, punishment for sin? "Perhaps" would be a good theological answer. In a general sense, suffering is a consequence for the sin of Adam and Eve, since suffering entered human history after their fall. When we turn to the possible link between specific sins and suffering the situation is more ambiguous. Does my sin cause my suffering? Yes and no. Some of my sins have specific consequences. If, for example, I am lazy and repeatedly refuse to do my work, I will be fired. Some actions do have very clear and obvious consequences.

Both testaments affirm a doctrine of retribution, that sometimes suffering is a direct consequence of sin.[11] One danger of this doctrine is its application to situations where it is not the right explanation for suffering. The book of Job, for example, is a critique of such an inappropriate use of the doctrine of retribution. Job's friends assumed that his suffering reflected his sin. Eliphaz asked Job, "Consider now: Who, being innocent, has ever perished?" (Job 4:7). These friends saw retribution as the only way to explain suffering. Like Job, they were in the dark about God allowing Satan to cause suffering to test Job's faith.

Jesus later affirmed that our actions do have consequences, but he warned against using the doctrine of retribution as the only clue to why humans suffer (Luke 13:1-5; John 9:1-3). Sin might lead to suffering, as in the story of the two men building homes. The wise man is rewarded, and the fool suffers a disaster in the storm (Matt. 7:24-27). But the rain falls on both the good and the bad people (Matt. 5:45).

The doctrine of retribution focuses on deserved suffering, but the Bible also recognizes that some suffering is innocent. Job was not sinless, but he knew he had not done anything to deserve the tragedies that struck him and his family.

I have a friend who has had Parkinson's disease for several years. No sin she committed is the cause for her disease. Although retribution may be useful as an explanation for some suffering, it is not the only way the Bible approaches human suffering. My sin might cause my suffering, but someone else's sin might be the cause.

If our suffering is due directly to our sin, then we need to confess that sin to God. Confession of sins is an essential element in Christian prayer, but in an age of self-deception such repentance may be difficult. A television ad for an alcohol treatment center explained that the alcoholic sometimes feels he is merely having "bad breaks." Eventually the alcoholic may realize that he is involved personally in the problem and will call for help.

If we are the victims of someone else's sin or see such a victim, we are obligated to respond as well. According to a friend, Dietrich Bonhoeffer said, "It is not only my task to look after the victims of madmen who drive a motorcar in a crowded street, but to do all in my power to stop their driving at all."[12] Christian prayer should help us sort out the source of our suffering and learn how to respond appropriately.

When You Walk Through the Fire

How do you respond to fires? Fire can be beneficial when it cooks our food or keeps us warm. But that same fire can be dangerous. A friend's house burned a few years ago when a wood-burning stove malfunctioned and his roof caught fire. The fire that warms can also wound.

The prophet Isaiah assured the Hebrews that "when you walk through the fire, you will not be burned" (Isa. 43:2).[13] If fire is a traditional symbol for suffering, how should we respond to such a fiery ordeal? We've already seen that, according to the concept of retribution, suffering might result from our sin. The pain of fire could be our deserved punishment, and we should repent. Can the pain of fire have other advantages for us? I believe suffering can have three positive aspects.

First, our suffering can lead to a better self-understanding. Whether the suffering is deserved or not, crises often compel us to review our basic priorities. A familiar old poem emphasized the possible learning associated with suffering.

> I walked a mile with Pleasure.
> She chattered all the way.
> But left me none the wiser
> For all she had to say.
>
> I walked a mile with Sorrow,
> And ne'er a word said she;
> But, oh, the things I learned from her
> When sorrow walked with me![14]

Such a testimony, however, usually comes in retrospect, after suffering's intensity has lessened. Such a sentiment may seem trite and glib to someone in the midst of sorrow or other forms of suffering. As we will see in the chapter on laments, we need to be honest in expressing our feelings to God. Also, those of us who try to minister to the suffering need to avoid trying to force them to learn some lesson from their experience too quickly.

Second, our suffering can lead us to deeper faith in God. When Job was experiencing the onslaught of tragedy, he doubted God's goodness. After God had appeared to him in the whirlwind, Job came to a deeper stage of faith. "My ears had heard of you but now my eyes have seen you" (Job 42:5).

God's testing or trying the faith of Job and Abraham reminds us that suffering can prompt a new, fresh awareness of God. Joseph concluded that the evil plans of his brothers were actually part of God's providence for his life (Gen. 50:20). C. S. Lewis noted that pain can be God's "megaphone to rouse a deaf world."[15]

Although foxhole experiences can be true learning experiences, not all sufferers gain a deeper insight into their relation to God. Some sufferers let the pain alienate them from God. Indeed, the issue of suffering frequently causes doubts either about God's character or existence. For example, blacks responded various ways to slavery. Some developed a form of black humanism and even asked if God were a white racist.[16]

Our prayers during our suffering need to be open and honest. If we try to deny our disappointment with God or our doubts, we may slide into agnosticism or atheism. Candid prayer to God and discussions with fellow Christians can help us gain insight into our suffering.

One value of Soelle's scheme of three stages to suffering is that it recognizes that our responses to suffering can change over time. A deeper understanding of ourselves and God may come through a process of reflection and prayer. As caregivers and sufferers, we should not expect all people to have these positive responses to suffering in a short time frame. Indeed, the suffering may be so severe and traumatic that a lifetime of prayer is needed to begin to see God's concern in the tragic events.

Third, suffering can be part of God's redemptive plans for God's people. One scholar noted that the Old Testament reveals three stages in its understanding of suffering, with the third stage, redemptive suffering, being the deepest insight.[17]

First, all sufferers are sinners, which was the view of Job's friends. You always get what you deserve. Second, some sufferers are saints, a view reflected by the book of Job. Here innocent suffering is granted as a possibility. Bad things do happen to good people. Third, some sufferers are saviors. This view is reflected in the suffering servant songs in Isaiah. The unnamed servant of the Lord would suffer innocently to bring about the salvation of sinners (Isa. 53:4-6).

The New Testament clearly used this third stage in its interpretation of the death of Jesus. Such innocent suffering can also be an effective part of the Christian's witness as well (1 Pet. 2:18-25). Peter told the Christian slaves that they should respond to unjust suffering by following Jesus' example of nonretaliation. Such behavior might be a persuasive witness to the unjust slave-owner.

A financial institution's ads often show a typical family facing some financial dilemma or decision. The slogan that concludes the ads is "Real life, real answers." In a much more profound way, Christian prayer acquaints us with the realities of life and provides real answers. Prayer is not an escape from the world. It is a genuine reflection on the realities of life in light of God's resources.

12

Prayer as Lament in an Age of Self-Control

"I'd rather do it myself!" Have you ever said that? Sometimes working with other people is so frustrating you would rather tackle the project by yourself. Narcissists often feel a strong need for control over a situation. They are especially bothered by situations such as temptation and suffering because life seems to have gotten out of their control. A character in the movie *The Bonfire of the Vanities* is described as master of the universe until his universe collapsed. Even for those of us who try to avoid the extreme self-centeredness of narcissism, the desire to control ourselves or some situation can be very powerful.

Our contemporary concern for control can be illustrated briefly from two areas of life. First, many of us assume that technology will eliminate much chaos from life and give us near total control over the negative side of existence. When the disease AIDS was first identified, the fear of death and an epidemic was rampant. An underlying concern was the realization that there was a medical problem that science could not solve easily. Disease and disasters trouble us because our technology, which seems omnipotent, shows its fallibility.

Second, advances in the field of psychology have offered the possibility of more control over inappropriate behavior. Behavior modification, for example, seems able to help alleviate behaviors judged harmful to the individual or to society. B. F. Skinner, a pioneer of behaviorism, even wrote a novel, *Walden Two*, about an ideal society based on his psychology. Rising crime rates and increasing violence seem, however, to belie the apparent control we have over ourselves and others.

The desire to provide relative order and stability to our lives is normal and beneficial. Narcissists, however, seem especially threatened when they cannot be in charge of a situation. A television ad for a mental health center shows an egg rolling aimlessly around a table while the narrator describes life's difficulties. As the egg rolls off the edge of the table, some hands, representing the care of the mental health facility, catch the egg. When your life seems out of control, how do you react? Where do you turn for help?

One common response is to turn inward and assert control over yourself. Perhaps unconsciously we say to ourselves, "Even if I can't control what happens around me, at least I can control myself and my response to the world around me."

One possible explanation for the increase in narcissism in recent decades is that it stems from the disillusionment of the social activists of the 1960s. When the civil rights and antiwar movements did not bring about the hoped for radical changes in American society, the theory says, people turned in on themselves. Concern for self replaced concern for society. A folk song of that generation echoes the concern to avoid involvement and pain by suggesting becoming a rock or an island.

This aspect of narcissism echoes the ancient Stoics, who exalted "apathy" (*apatheia*) or emotionlessness as a proper response to life's difficulties. Rather than reacting emotionally to the ups and downs of life, they recommended a rational, reflective approach to life as a way to maintain control over the chaos that surrounded them.[1]

Instead of inward self-control, biblical figures and writers frequently are open and candid about their negative feelings. Normally they address these feelings to God rather than suppressing them. Rather than denying the existence of God, the biblical writer would often wrestle with the issue of the character of God. For instance, Habakkuk dialogued with God about why a good God would allow the impending invasion of Judah by an evil nation (Hab. 1:2-17). Even when they felt the absence of God more than his presence, the believers prayed to God.

A lament is the type of biblical prayer that fits this mood of concern about the difficulties of life.[2] A lament is a complaint or a statement of dissatisfaction about life. The book of Lamentations in the Old Testament reflects the situation of the Hebrews during the period of the Babylonian exile. As a defeated nation, they were disappointed with God and felt abandoned and helpless. Jerusalem resembles a widow who has no one to comfort her (Lam. 1:1-2). The people know that their suffering was deserved but still were troubled by their sad situation. Similar discontent resounds through the "confessions" of Jeremiah.[3] Jeremiah felt so alienated from his people, who would not listen to his message, that he complained to God and wished he had never been born (Jer. 20:14).

Laments are plentiful in the book of Psalms. The psalmists frequently voice their concerns to God in frank and vivid prayers. Psalm 69, for example, begins with the writer saying he is up to his neck in trouble (Ps. 69:1-2). A typical lament includes a statement of the complaint as well as an expression of confidence that God will indeed respond to the situation.

Laments sometimes sound harsh to us because of the apparent self-righteousness of the psalmist. Although the writer sometimes mentions his sinfulness, more often he protests that he is the innocent victim of an injustice. At heart the laments are anguished cries for God to exercise justice in the world.[4] Even when the writer pleads for God to do some terrible things to the writer's enemies, the context makes it clear that the justice is God's. Although some of the requests seem vindictive to us, we can appreciate the psalmist's honesty in his prayer to God.

The lament type of prayer typically occurs in those times when we feel the absence of God. When life is positive and upbeat, thanksgiving and praise seem natural. When we are vividly aware of our sins, confession is an appropriate prayer. When we feel abandoned by God, lament is the most honest prayer.

The darkening of the sun during an eclipse symbolizes the low points of life. All you can see is the penumbra, the ring of light around the darkness caused by the moon. When people experience the eclipse of God, they need to be reminded that God is only temporarily hidden from view.[5] A superficial optimism ignores the prayer of lament and encourages self-deception about the realities of life.

The Power of Negative Thinking

A prayer life without laments would probably be dishonest, since people normally feel a sense of injustice at some time in life. But this type of material can lead to "a neurotic preoccupation with self and focuses too much attention on everything bad."[6] Certainly if lament becomes the primary form of prayer, the temptation is to wallow in self-pity. In this section we will try to sketch the salient features of a Christian view of life.

How would you finish the sentence "Life is_____"? Trying to summarize your view of life in a word or phrase may be impossible, but writers of proverbs, graffiti, and bumper stickers realize that something can be said in a few words.

A T-shirt said, "Life is uncertain . . . so eat dessert first." In the "Beetle Bailey" cartoon Beetle complained during one military exercise, with bullets flying overhead, that this activity could be fatal. His friend responded "Life is always fatal." Beetle thought that attitude was very depressing!

A Christian psychologist began his book, "Life is difficult."[7] An athletic shoe company notes, "life is not a spectator sport." A radio humorist said, "Life is complicated and not for the timid."[8]

The traditional options we consider for evaluating views of life such as these are optimism, pessimism, and realism. Optimism stresses the positive events of life, and pessimism highlights the negative experiences. Realism claims to provide a balanced view of the positive and negative features of life. Compared to the perspectives of many movies and novels, the Christian view of life is the most realistic. The Christian faith is most willing to acknowledge life in all of its complexity without glossing over its difficulties and overstating its pleasures. Optimism and pessimism are cousins—they both are superficial and extrapolate beyond the evidence.[9]

Realism is a useful category for evaluating trends in our culture. For example, the television series "M*A*S*H" was realistic about human experience. In one episode Hawkeye Pierce was very upset that a friend died on the operating table. As a surgeon in the Korean war, Hawkeye had seen a lot of young men die, but his friend's death brought real grief.

Henry Blake tried to console Hawkeye by mentioning two "rules" he had learned. First, young men die in war. Second, doctors can't change rule number one. Full of youthful optimism, Hawkeye had assumed that he could stop the death of his friend. Through events such as the death of his friend he learned to be more realistic about life.

An unrealistic view of life dictates that justice always prevails (optimism) or that injustice is universal (pessimism). In our normal human experience, the good and the bad are mixed together. The famous opening words of Ecclesiastes 3 remind us of the complexities of life.

> There is a time for everything, and a season for every activity under heaven: a time to be born and a time to die (Eccles. 3:1-2).

Life typically brings birth and death, joy and sorrow, and many other experiences. Koheleth does not mean that we are fated to experience all of these, but in the normal course of life most of these will come to most of us. Jesus told his followers that the rain falls on the just and the unjust (Matt. 5:45). On the cross Jesus cried, "My God, my God, why have you forsaken me?" (Mark 15:34). One writer noted that those words were the genuine Lord's Prayer.[10] Although the resurrection was only a few days away, Jesus experienced the agony of the absence of God.

One way to recover a healthy realism in our Christian life is to compare three views of *eschatology*, the doctrine of last things. Without reviewing the vast scholarly literature on the subject, we can summarize them briefly. Each view of the end of time has definite implications for the way we live and pray today.

First, some think that all the pleasures and rewards of the end of time should be available today. Sometimes the advocates of the so-called health and wealth gospel seem to suggest that all of the blessings of heaven should be possessed by Christians now.

When Charlie Brown shares his sandwich with his pet dog, Snoopy, he comments, "I can tell you it just doesn't get any better than this!"

Snoopy thinks to himself, "It doesn't?"

The Bible does not promise that all the negative experiences of life will disappear in this life for Christians. Total elimination of the dark side of life awaits the end of time (Rev. 21:1-5). A false optimism hints we can have this heaven on earth now, but Snoopy's reaction is sound. It does get better. A false optimism reflects a realized eschatology that leaves no room for significant action by God in the future.

Second, some think that life here is totally bleak and nothing good will happen until God dramatically changes the course of history. In this apocalyptic perspective, life is grim and full of trouble.

In one comic strip the son asked, "Dad, what do you call a man who thinks the whole world is against him?"

His father responded, "A realist."

Such a view borders on pessimism or cynicism. Christians who hold this view imply that God has totally abandoned God's people until the end of time. Jesus, however, promised that he would always be with us (Matt. 28:19-20).

Third, a truly realistic view of life recognizes the good and the bad experiences of ordinary human existence. The movie *Places in the Heart* reminds us of the balance between the realities of our life today and the transformation at the end of time. After the movie dealt realistically with the struggle of a young widow to harvest a crop and save her farm, the movie ended with a communion service. In it, her dead husband, now strangely alive, and his murderer both participated. The reconciliation they shared anticipates the end of time, not real life today.

A classic illustration of this realistic view of life involves the difference between D-Day and V-Day in World War II.[11] D-Day was the turning point in the war, but the peace treaty was not signed until months later. Between D-Day and V-Day the fighting continued, but the outcome of the war was assured. As Christians we live between D-Day, the death and resurrection of Jesus, and V-Day, the return of Christ. We are assured that God is the victor over the forces of evil, but we will not see the full fruition of that victory until the end of time. We live in the time between the already and the not yet.[12]

An authentic prayer life should reflect a realistic view of life. If we pray out of a false optimism, we will be repeatedly disappointed, for we will expect things to happen now that await the end of time. If we pray from a false pessimism, then we will be resigned to less than God has to offer here and now. Life is difficult, but our prayer life can echo our confidence that God has not abandoned us. A strong dose of negative thinking might help to correct superficial positive thinking. Genuinely Christian prayer travels the middle road between the two extremes.

Don't Do It Yourself Without Us

An ad for a hardware store advised: "Don't do it yourself without us." At first I was puzzled because the slogan seemed to be a contradiction in terms. If you do something on your own, I thought, then you don't need any help. I realized, of course, that they would provide the materials and expertise for a do-it-yourself project.

That slogan provides a rough analogy for how to live a Christian life in the midst of a very real world. Since we live between D-Day and V-Day, we await the final realization of the kingdom of God. We are not, however, on our own since God has provided a number of resources for living between the times.

First, God has promised to be present with us in our times of temptation and testing. Paul described God as "the Father of compassion and the God of all comfort" (2 Cor. 1:3). As the Father of compassion, God identifies with us in our adversity. God is not aloof and distant from us; rather, God is Immanuel, God with us. God is the God of all comfort because God is actively involved in addressing our pain and suffering.

When Jesus prayed for his disciples, he did not ask God to exempt them from suffering but asked God to protect them (John 17:15). Being a Christian does not make us immune from all of the problems intrinsic to being a human, but we are assured of God's compassion and comfort.

A second resource for our life in this world is the continuing presence of the risen Jesus. Sometimes we stress the return of Christ so much that we forget he promised to be with us until the end of the age (Matt. 28:20). In the upper room, Jesus knew that his disciples were troubled about his imminent departure. He assured them that their relationship would not end simply because of his physical absence. He would not leave them orphans (John 14:18).

A third resource for contemporary Christian living is the Holy Spirit. Jesus told his followers that the *paraclete* would be with them after he left (John 14:15-18). This Greek word means someone called alongside to help you. When these early disciples faced adversity, they would have the Holy Spirit by their side to help them. Paul later echoed this note, affirming that the Holy Spirit would help weak Christians (Rom. 8:26).

A fourth resource is the Christian community, the church. Paul often noted how other Christians had comforted and assisted him in his ministry (2 Cor. 7:6-7). Indeed, God comforts us so we can comfort others (2 Cor. 1:4). When we face wintry times, the warm fellowship of other Christians sustains us.

Uncle Charlie on the old television series "My Three Sons" told the boys, "Life is a real bumpy road. What you've got to develop is real good shock absorbers." In this life the bumps and bruises will continue, even for Christians, but we do not face these struggles alone. We have valuable resources, or shock absorbers if you please, for the trials and temptations of life.

The famous "Serenity Prayer" by Reinhold Niebuhr epitomizes the realistic view of life characteristic of the Christian faith.[13] "O God, give us the serenity to accept what cannot be changed, courage to change what should be changed, and wisdom to distinguish the one from the other."

When we pray for avoidance of temptation and deliverance from evil, as Jesus instructed, we do not expect the total elimination of all adversity. The Serenity Prayer reminds us we can change some aspects of our world, but others resist change. We need the wisdom to know the difference.

13

This Is Living!

Have you ever met a narcissist? According to Richard Foster, narcissism "is the dominant mood of our age."[1] One trouble with any "ism" is that such ideal types do not always match our lived experience. If you cannot think of a concrete example of narcissism, then the issue of "Christ and Narcissus" may seem esoteric or unimportant.

Defined in simple terms, a narcissist is someone who is self-centered. More precisely, narcissism is an unhealthy preoccupation with self that distorts a person's relationship to God, other people, nature, and oneself.

Narcissism does not always, however, appear in a bold, brash form. It would be easy, for example, to confuse Narcissus and Prometheus. In Greek legend Prometheus challenged the gods by stealing fire and bringing it to mankind. Zeus chained him to a rock, where a vulture ate his liver each day.

Prometheus might well represent dictators such as Hitler or others who are egocentric manipulators of people. The more extreme forms of social activism in the 1960s might have been Promethean in tone, but Narcissus is the idol for a quieter, more conservative generation that has turned inward. Reflecting on his theological pilgrimage, William Willimon noted that "Narcissus has replaced Prometheus as our idol."[2]

By placing self at the center of life, a narcissist demonstrates a disregard for other people and for God but may not consciously challenge God's authority. Rather, narcissists may simply live as if there is no God. Narcissism affects our culture in subtle ways. Looking out for yourself as number one may not make you a brash, obnoxious person. You may become quietly and politely self-centered.

A popular limerick captures the essence of the Greek legend about Narcissus.

> There once was a nymph named Narcissus,
> Who thought himself delicious;
> So he stared like a fool
> At his face in a pool,
> And his folly today is still with us.[3]

Ebenezer Scrooge in Charles Dickens' classic, *A Christmas Carol*, fits the narcissist's profile, not because he is necessarily anti-God or antireligion, but because he has limited his concerns to himself. He is not sensitive to the poor, not even those he employs. Like his dead business partner, Jacob Marley, his life revolves around himself and his money.

A narcissist puts self before other people, God, or the physical world. Narcissism is evident in the request of James and John to have places of prominence in Jesus' kingdom (Mark 10:35-45). They wanted to "be first" in the kingdom (Mark 10:44).

The attitude of the narcissist is epitomized in a television commercial for house paint. Several representatives of paint companies nervously await the outcome of a scientific test of their products. When the scientist announces which company is first, one of the also-rans asks, "Who came in second?" The scientist's response is classic narcissism. "Does it really matter?" To narcissists being first is all-important.

In this chapter we explore two issues crucial to a Christian response to narcissism. First is the cluster of issues related to self-fulfillment and self-love. Can there be genuine self-fulfillment through narcissism? And does the Christian faith allow for self-love? Second is the relation of prayer to the totality of the Christian life. Is prayer an integral part of Christian living, or is it a luxury for a busy, active Christian?

Prayer in an Age of Self-Fulfillment

Why has narcissism been so popular in recent decades? Several factors may have contributed to its recent vitality. First, recent preoccupation with self may reflect disenchantment with the social activism of the 1960s. The 1960s and early 1970s saw social activism focused on issues such as civil rights, the Vietnam conflict, and ecology. When these problems seemed resistant to social change, personal concerns took center stage.

When Charlie Brown noted that young people did not seem to have any causes, Lucy exclaimed, "I believe in *me*! I'm my *own* cause!" Self needs rather than societal needs became the focus of attention.

Second, recent narcissism may be the intensification of our typical American individualism and self-reliance. The frontier mentality that helped the early European settlers of this country may be reexpressing itself.

Third, narcissism may be the fixation of our behavior at an infantile stage. If growing up means a life of duty and discipline, then childhood can seem quite appealing. Like Peter Pan, we might prefer to stay young rather than growing older.

Fourth, theologians could cite pride as one of the basic forms of human sin. Selfishness or self-worship is a major dimension, if not the essence, of pride. As our culture has grown more secular, pride manifests itself more widely.

Is God Selfish?

Although these explanations and others have validity, narcissism may also be understood as a reaction to a common misunderstanding of the Christian faith. Narcissism is partly a response to the presentation of the Christian faith in one-sided terms as self-denial. Self-denial is integral to the Christian faith, but many contemporary Americans apparently do not hear its biblical meaning. To a narcissist, self-denial conflicts with self-fulfillment.

Use your imagination to think of the most degrading, humiliating relationship possible between human beings. Slavery, wife abuse, and child abuse are possible answers. In the old television series "All in the Family," for example, Archie Bunker consistently put down his wife, Edith. Although he may have sincerely loved her, he often told her to "stifle yourself."

In the comic strip "Blondie," Dagwood Bumstead works for an employer who is dictatorial and domineering. In one episode the boss announces to the employees, "It's not whether you win or lose that counts. It's whether or not *I* win or lose." We may smile at these fictional scenes—but would try to avoid them in real life.

Narcissism is partly a reaction against such unilateral, dehumanizing relationships. The narcissist assumes, falsely, that the God of Christians sees humans as rivals who must fall prostrate before their divine tyrant. The preconscious image of God that operates for many people is something like Big Brother in George Orwell's novel *1984*. God seems a divine despot intent on humiliating people. God expects people to be God's robots. God demands our adulation because of a need for psychological reinforcement.

Is God an egotist? Does God want our praise because God is selfish? Christians respond that God deserves our praise because of God's intrinsic worth. Worship is based on the acknowledgment of real value. God is "not a petty tyrant who requires flattery and regular ego-pampering."[4]

Narcissism misunderstands praise and prayer because it fails to recognize the God-centered nature of the universe. Because a narcissist is preoccupied with self, he or she suspects that God must operate from the same perspective. To a narcissist everyone else is a rival, so God must be the supreme rival.

To a narcissist the available options for life seem to be autonomy or heteronomy. "Autonomy," from the Greek words for self (*autos*) and law (*nomos*), refers to someone who is self-ruled or self-governed. The narcissist believes that the only route to self-fulfillment is through total self rule. "I did it my way" could be the theme song for a narcissist. To live by someone else's standards or expectations would be humiliating and enslaving.

The only alternative to autonomy the narcissist seems to see is heteronomy. Here the law comes from the "other" (*heteros*). The narcissist assumes that the other would be an oppressive, restrictive person, idea, or institution.

Unfortunately, Christianity has sometimes played the role of denier of human freedom. Dostoevski's fictional "Grand Inquisitor" told Jesus that the church had used "miracle, mystery, and authority" to suppress people after Jesus had offered them freedom.[5] Institutional religion has sometimes been guilty of being authoritarian and heteronomous. Narcissists need to realize that such an oppressive version of Christianity is a distortion of Jesus' mission. Jesus is liberator, not enslaver.

The Christian faith actually offers *theonomy* as a third option transcending autonomy and heteronomy.[6] Theonomy is the orientation of life to God's rule or law. Stated that bluntly, the narcissist will suspect that Christian legalism is being slipped in by the back door. In fact, theonomy allows for both the sovereignty of God and human self-fulfillment.

The key to accepting theonomy is the basic image of God. As long as God is perceived as a tyrant, the notion of law or rule will sound oppressive. When we realize that God is Father and Friend rather than Foe, then we see that our relationship to God is not restrictive or limiting. God's authority is not capricious or arbitrary; rather, God intends the best for us.

True self-fulfillment comes through a vital relationship with God. God's expectations of us actually contribute to our fulfillment because God created us and wants what is right for us. Freedom is not unrestricted, individualistic autonomy. Christian freedom is the experience of release from every hindrance to personal self-fulfillment and peaceful social interaction. And freedom is the realization of a developing relationship with God. Rugged individualism is not only lonely; it actually stifles human fulfillment. Being truly human means living in harmony with God, not a false antagonism with a divine despot.

The classic statement by Jesus on the divine-human relationship is the parable of the prodigal son (Luke 15:11-32). The father did not veto the younger son's decision to leave home with his inheritance. He exercised his parental authority by lovingly letting his son go.

Our popular conceptions of power usually focus on brute force or the manipulation of someone. God's power as Father, however, operates on the model of relationships. To control someone else physically reflects less real power than lovingly wooing them.

Here the emphasis of process theology on divine power as loving persuasion rather than coercion would help alleviate the narcissist's concern about being manipulated by God.[7] A God on an ego-trip might be possessive of God's creatures and control their lives. As a loving Father and Friend, God allows them finite freedom. God creates and sustains us through a loving, non-coercive relationship. God's self-giving, non-tyrannical love deserves our praise.

How to Love Yourself Without Being a Narcissist

Advertisements for many products and organizations encourage us to be the best we can. The language of self-fulfillment and self-actualization permeates our culture, making the Christian emphasis on self-denial and loving others sound alien. A narcissistic culture seems to promise true self-fulfillment while Christianity seems to offer self-destruction. In this section we will explore these rival claims.[8]

In previous chapters we noted some traits of extreme egocentrism. Although a narcissist might manifest only one or two of these traits, they constitute a constellation of characteristics that pervade our popular culture. First, a narcissist feels love of self is a duty. Any obligation to other people, even family or friends, tends to be a nuisance or a distraction from the primary concern: self.

Second, a narcissist practices self-assertiveness. Since other people are perceived as rivals and fellow narcissists, you can get ahead only by aggressively insisting on what is rightfully yours. Looking out for number one means playing "king of the mountain" past childhood.

Third, narcissism entails an attitude of self-sufficiency. Any dependency on other people must be kept to a minimum. Controlling your own destiny is crucial.

Fourth, a narcissist has to practice self-deception. Admitting to inadequacies or failures is detrimental to the illusion of being invulnerable.

Fifth, a narcissist seeks total self-control. A narcissist is threatened by crises or chaos.

Can Christians love themselves without being narcissists? Some writers pose the issue in terms of a stark contrast. The choice, they say, is between loving self or loving God, between self-love or selfless love.

In a helpful analysis, Gene Outka suggests a spectrum of four views held by Christians of the validity of self-love.[9] First, some Christians assert that all self-love is wholly nefarious. Self-love is totally rejected because it is based on the sin of pride. The primary concern of life is acquiring things for oneself.

Second, some insist that self-love is normal, reasonable, and prudent. Self-love is not necessarily bad or good but simply a natural part of human behavior. Self-love so understood is compatible with love of neighbor.

Third, self-love is actually one way to love others. When we love and look out for ourselves, for example, we avoid becoming a burden on others.

Fourth, some Christians insist that self-love is a definite obligation. Self-love in the sense of self-respect and a healthy self-esteem is desirable for Christians.

Christian discussions of the propriety of self-love focus on a few key biblical texts. When Jesus was asked to identify the great command, he cited two: love God and love your neighbor as yourself (Matt. 22:37-39). This second command raises the issue of self-love. Jesus did not say to love your neighbor instead of yourself, but did he mean that we have an obligation to love ourselves? Jesus could be saying, "You ought to love others as you (*ought to*) love yourself," or perhaps, "You ought to love others as you do (*in fact*) love yourselves."[10]

Either way, self-love seems to be tacitly approved. Still, critics of self-love note that there is no explicit command in Scripture for loving yourself. At best self-love is assumed or implied in this text.

Although this commandment might allow for self-love, narcissists object to other passages that encourage self-denial. True fulfillment, they insist, cannot include putting yourself down. Self-expression, not self-denial, is essential to self-actualization. We have already looked at the fear that God is a tyrant as one factor in the popularity of narcissism. Another related factor seems to be a fear that concern for others would be detrimental to personal fulfillment. The narcissist says in effect, "If I get involved in your needs and problems, then I won't have any energy for myself. It takes all of my time and resources just keeping my act together."

The narcissist, perhaps unconsciously, sees only two options: a pure, autonomous self or total annihilation of self. The pure self requires a total investment of energies for developing and maintaining personal identity. Commitment to other people would, on the other hand lead to a complete diminishment of self. If I love others or help others, I'll lose my identity.

For example, a young woman might reject marriage and the possibility of motherhood out of the fear that she would only be Tom's wife or Sally's mother. She would have no personal identity. A narcissist would typically choose to be a self-maximizer rather than a covenant-keeper.[11]

Addressing marriage, Lewis Smedes comments that self-maximizers evaluate that relationship in terms of its contribution to personal growth. Is the relationship helping me? A covenant-keeper realizes that life involves more than self-growth.

Narcissists tend to think of personal identity in an atomistic, individualistic manner. Christians, however, see personal identity in terms of relationships. I am who I am because I am related to other people and God. Paul echoes this from a prison cell (Phil. 1:21-26). His personal preference would be to die and be with God, but he knows it would be better for him to continue to serve others. He is not on his own and he is not his own (see 1 Cor. 6:19-20).

When narcissists attempt to focus their lives totally on personal needs and desires, they often feel a sense of frustration rather than fulfillment. In *The Great Divorce* C. S. Lewis depicted the inhabitants of hell as mere shadows and the inhabitants of heaven as solid people.[12] The selfishness of the sinners had caused their loss of reality, while those in heaven had reality and identity. Real fulfillment in life comes from relationships with God and other people, not from isolation. Being number one can be very lonely and unfulfilling.

Jesus said that whoever really wants to find his life must lose it (Matt. 16:25-26; John 12:24). John added that if we fail to love others, we are still dead (1 John 3:14). A narcissist may claim to be truly alive, but preoccupation with self really produces spiritual deadness. Concern for others brings fulfillment, not diminishment of self. "Self-expenditure is self-fulfillment."[13]

Narcissism reflects a possessive attitude characteristic of a child. In a comic strip a little girl comes home complaining, "Kindergarten is always the same thing: sharing, sharing, sharing. . . ." If we want to keep everything for ourselves, sharing is frustrating. If we realize our fulfillment comes from meaningful relationships with God and others, then sharing is natural.

One Christmas a father in a comic strip tells his family he wants a new sword, a fishing rod, and a keg of ale for Christmas. His son asks for peace on earth, his wife wishes for the elimination of poverty everywhere, and his daughter asks for more love in the world. Realizing how selfish he had been, the father asks, "Is it too late for me to change my selections?" He sees that his family's wishes are more appropriate for a season dedicated to Christ and giving.

Self-love provides the total orientation for life for a narcissist, but a Christian understands legitimate self-love as one component in a hierarchy of loves. Bernard of Clairvaux in the twelfth century proposed a scheme of four stages of self-love.[14] First, we love ourselves for self's sake. Second, we love God for self's sake. Third, we love God for God's sake. Fourth, we love self for God's sake.

The narcissism we have examined in this study is closest to the first level. Narcissists often assume that Christians affirm only step three, loving God without any concern for self. Ideally, we reach stage four in which we realize that we are God's loved creatures.

As Christians we can legitimately love ourselves in a variety of ways. Fulfillment for the Christian means maturing in all areas of life. Luke's brief summaries of Jesus' development are a helpful set of criteria for human development as well. "And the child grew and became strong; he was filled with wisdom, and the grace of God was upon him" (Luke 2:40). "And Jesus grew in wisdom and stature, and in favor with God and men" (Luke 2:52).

Jesus matured in his relationship to God and others, physically and emotionally. By devoting himself to God and other people, he realized personal fulfillment. Physical fitness, social relations, and intellectual development as well as spiritual concerns all are important to human fulfillment.

Prayer, Problem-Solving, and Priorities

What would you do if you only had a short time to live? Cartoonists frequently note the odd priorities we seem to have by incorporating the end of the world as a theme. When one cartoon character sees a man carrying a sign announcing the world will end soon, he asks, "Do I have time for a pepperoni pizza?" In another comic strip, a child responds to a similar sign by sadly noting, "Just my luck. I already did my homework."

We have already seen a variety of possible reasons for the popularity of narcissism in our culture. Disillusionment with the results of the social activism of the 1960s and a misconception of God as a tyrant were among the options.

Another possibility is that Americans, despite a superficial affluence, are fearful of the threat of scarcity. While the elderly may recall the economic depression of the 1930s, members of the postwar baby boom recall the discussion of the threat of nuclear war in the 1950s. Some people in my town built bomb shelters in the anticipation of nuclear attack.

One ethical issue frequently raised was how a family might respond to someone who wanted into their shelter. If you built a shelter and stocked it with food adequate for your family, could you admit anyone else? To share your space and your food would endanger your family. To exclude these desperate people would be selfish. Self-preservation and Christian humanitarianism seemed to clash.

Narcissism might be a response to the threat of reduced or

limited resources. "What's mine is mine!" becomes appealing when time or resources are limited. It's easy to share when there is plenty to go around, but the choice is more difficult when there's not much for anyone. Recent discussions of "lifeboat ethics" involve the same dynamics about the tension between taking care of one's self and concern for others. If too many people are allowed in the lifeboat, then all will die.[15]

In this section we will look at two aspects of Christian prayer. First, we examine the relation of prayer to problem-solving. Prayer is not a luxury, separated from real life; prayer is extremely relevant to our daily decision-making. Second, we will look at prayer as an integral component of a meaningful, fulfilled life. The way we pray and the way we live are intimately intertwined. Our priorities are influenced and shaped by what we pray.

Prayer and Problem-Solving

The issue of relevance seems paramount to most of us. "So what?" is a predictable response to any idea. If an idea has no immediate relevance, then we see no need to spend our time with it. Christian prayer is relevant to our lives in many ways, but in this section we will highlight its significance for problem-solving.[16] "Life is a series of problems," and the Christian needs to develop problem-solving skills.[17]

As Christians we need to approach problems from a distinctively Christian standpoint. Since we live in a world populated with many authorities and experts, we need to base our decisions on the resources of the Christian faith. Expediency, pragmatism, and materialism might be attractive criteria for narcissistic problem-solvers—but we need to practice *Christian* problem-solving.

Although Christians normally grant some authority to reason, empirical studies, and church tradition, our primary authority should be the Bible interpreted in the context of our church community. Even when the Bible does not explicitly tackle some issue, we can discern principles that will guide our decisions.

Christian problem-solving requires cultivation of a genuine Christian concern for contemporary issues. Narcissists, having turned inward, focus on their personal needs and desires. Christians need to be more other-directed. Prayer tunes us in to the priorities of God for his kingdom; prayer becomes, in effect, a form of consciousness-raising for Christians.

Prayer should help us overcome the ignorance and apathy that often accompany narcissism. "I don't know and I don't care" should not characterize a Christian who prays with the Lord's Prayer as the pattern for life.

Our concern for the world, shaped by Christian prayer, will be comprehensive, acknowledging a wide range of contemporary issues. Unfortunately, some Christians wait until an issue has reached crisis proportions before they address it. Like narcissists, they wait until an issue touches them personally before they are concerned with it. Pollution of water and air, for example, might be low priority issues until they reach my city or home. Too often our response is reactive rather than proactive. Prayer should help us cultivate a global consciousness that transcends our natural provincialism and ethnocentrism.

Prayer should also help us understand the complexity of many of today's problems. In my ethics classes I use case studies to encourage students to see the many facets of moral dilemmas. On the chalkboard I list three categories to be considered for each case study—values, options, and others who count. In each of these categories I hope they will see several possibilities. Even if we do not always agree on what the central character in the case should do, we generally recognize the complexity of the choice he or she is confronting.

Prayer, especially in public worship, reminds us of the interrelation of character and community. Although narcissists only acknowledge individual decisions, Christians see the value of the community of faith for decision-making. Two heads are better than one is often true in Christian decision-making. My decisions are shaped by my family, friends, co-workers, and church.

A comprehensive prayer life set within the context of the community of faith will keep me conscious not only of the needs to be addressed but the insights of these other people. Praying with a Christian agenda in the company of fellow Christians will increase the likelihood of our developing a Christlike character.

Prayer will also help us overcome the so-called "paralysis of analysis." My students sometimes become so adept at analyzing an issue or problem that they fail to reach a decision and act on it. Fearful of overlooking another aspect to the issue, they become paralyzed. Lewis Smedes appropriately entitled one of his chapters in *Choices*, "When You Can't Be Sure, Be Responsible."[18] Absolute certainty may not characterize our problem-solving, but we must nevertheless courageously implement our decisions.

Attention to the probable consequences of our actions is another concern of genuine prayer. Prayer should not engender simplistic analyses or simple solutions to life's problems. Prayer should give us a realistic appraisal of what the problems are and the probable consequences of our actions. A narcissist typically asks, "What's in it for me?" Christians also want to know about the consequences of an action. But they will do the right thing even if it does not lead to personal acclaim or reward.

Christian prayer aids in problem-solving, but not by being one step among many steps. Rather, prayer is essential throughout the process of addressing problems.

Make Us Truly Alive

What do you really want? What is your deepest desire? Recent interest in self-actualization and self-expression probably reflects a perennial concern for achieving a full, meaningful life. An early church leader prayed, "We beg you, make us truly alive."[19]

Joseph Campbell, a student of world religions, suggested that what we all want "is an experience of being alive . . . so that we actually feel the rapture of being alive."[20] Narcissists, who want to have it all, fear that the Christian faith is life-denying. A television ad for low-calorie food includes the slogan, "This is living!" Losing weight may be essential to good physical health for some, but real living is not found through dieting alone. Likewise, narcissism is not the right path to true life.

In this section we will stress the value of prayer for making us truly alive. Rather than being a pious extra added to a full life, prayer is essential to living life to its fullest. Indeed, how we pray shapes who we are and how we live. Jennings' comment that "liturgy shapes lifestyle" is not an overstatement.[21] What we say to God and what he says to us does shape our view of life.

An old Latin aphorism, *lex orandi, lex credendi* ("law of praying, law of believing"), points to the interdependence of prayer and theology.[22] Our prayers do reflect what we believe, and our deepest convictions determine what we say in prayer. Likewise, what we pray shapes all of our life, not just our beliefs. Using an expanded version of this aphorism, Willimon notes,

> The *lex orandi, lex credendi, lex bene operandi* (law of prayer, law of belief, law of good work) are all part of Christians' response to God. We speak and listen, believe in and trust, and imitate whom we adore. Our praying, believing, and good deeds are three mutually enriching ways of responding to the God who first loved us in Jesus Christ.[23]

Prayer, then, is an integral part of life for the Christian striving to live a rich, authentic life.

"Pray without ceasing" (1 Thes. 5:17, NRSV) puzzles us as long as we think of prayer as something we do for a few minutes a day. How can we pray all of the time? The praying has to stop, we assume, so we can get on with real life. By contrast, Paul's concern was to remind us that what we pray is not separated from the rest of life. To pray constantly does not mean ignoring the real world. Authentic Christian prayer touches life at its center, not its circumference.

Our study highlighted the concerns of the Lord's Prayer as a model for prayer and the whole of the Christian life. Each of those concerns should permeate our lives even when we are not consciously "praying." I do not mean to blur the boundary between prayer and everything else we do, but too often we draw a sharp dividing line between our piety and the rest of life. What we say before the "Amen," and what we do after the "Amen" should be consistent. Our worship does not end with the "Amen."

A Christian life, shaped by the Model Prayer, will include five concerns. First, prayer puts us in touch with the God revealed in Jesus. In a culture that promotes a large pantheon of gods, we must pray to "Our Father."

Second, we will make God's kingdom the central value in our value system. We can make our petitions to God, knowing that our priorities should coincide with God's priorities. Praying that God's kingdom will come and God's will be done protects us from making our pet projects the center of our lives.

Third, our lives will manifest gratitude for the gifts of God. When we are tempted to think we are self-made people, the Model Prayer provides the corrective of knowing that our "bread" is a gift from God.

Fourth, praying for forgiveness of our sins may be painful, especially if we are prone to practice self-deception or to blame others for our faults. Realizing that God forgives us should motivate us to be forgiving in our relations with others.

Fifth, prayer energizes us for life in a real world. Prayer is not a defense mechanism or a form of escapism. Rather, praying prepares us for the struggle with temptation and evil.

The early Christian prayed correctly, "We beg you, make us truly alive." The praying and the becoming alive are interrelated events. As we pray in a truly Christian way, we will be fully alive. Indeed the praying puts us in touch with the source of genuine life, the God revealed in Jesus of Nazareth.

14

Prayer as Transformation of Self

How can a Christian avoid the influence of narcissism? Is narcissism so prevalent in North American culture that it inevitably taints us? Paul wrote, "Don't let the world around you squeeze you into its own mold, but let God remold your minds from within" (Rom. 12:2, Phillips). Shortly after this, Paul mentioned a false estimate of self-worth as a danger sign for the Roman Christians. "Do not think of yourself more highly than you ought" (Rom. 12:3).

When Christians become sensitive to the tension between Christ and Narcissus, they will look for ways to avoid being squeezed into a narcissistic mold by our culture. Narcissism is "in the air." Christians cannot avoid confronting it.

A central thesis of this study is that Christian prayer, guided by the petitions of the Lord's Prayer, is a valuable resource in responding to narcissism. The Lord's Prayer epitomizes many of the central values and convictions of the Christian faith. Praying as Jesus taught his early disciples will help contemporary disciples avoid becoming narcissists. A consistent, disciplined life of

Christian praying will help us to become more Christlike and less vulnerable to a narcissistic worldview.

In this chapter we will treat three interrelated issues. First, we will focus on the type of experiences that might cause a narcissist to consider Christ as an alternative to Narcissus. Second, we will see how God has consistently taken the initiative to transform those who have followed an egocentric lifestyle rather than a Christ-centered lifestyle. Third, we will examine the transforming power of Christian prayer. A Christlike character or personal identity is one effect of a life oriented and directed by Christian prayer.

When All You've Ever Wanted Isn't Enough

Commenting on the book of Ecclesiastes, John Paterson noted that there are two kinds of disappointment.[1] First, you might strive to reach a goal but be disappointed when you never reach it. Second, you might reach your goal but be disappointed that your goal does not bring real satisfaction. Having tried to find meaning for his life in a variety of activities, Koheleth experienced the second type of disappointment.

Paterson identifies one source of Koheleth's dissatisfaction as narcissism. "The Preacher is suffering from 'I' trouble. Life is centered in self: he is an egoist."[2] If we take Koheleth's disappointment as a clue to the experience of narcissists, we realize why Harold Kushner titled his study of Ecclesiastes *When All You've Ever Wanted Isn't Enough*. Kushner asks, "To what question is God the answer?"[3] The thesis of this section is that thoughtful narcissists will eventually see God as the answer to their search for meaning. Narcissism is the question, not the answer.

Some narcissists might feel enough satisfaction with an egocentric orientation to life to maintain a longterm commitment to it. They might theoretically never become restless or look for a better value system. The witness of Scripture and personal experience indicates, however, that many narcissists will eventually grow weary of narcissism and look for a more satisfying lifestyle.

Some commentators on Ecclesiastes suggest that Koheleth's quest for contentment and meaning in life can only be adequately answered by Christ. Ecclesiastes demonstrates "the barrenness of egoism" and is "a *Preparatio evangelica*."[4] Early in his *Confessions* Augustine comments that "our hearts are restless until they find peace in you."[5]

For some narcissists, then, there comes a time when their egocentrism becomes a problem or question rather than a solution to life's problems. Like the popular song title, the question becomes "Is that all there is?"

What might prompt a narcissist to begin looking beyond narcissism for more meaning to life? Two possible scenarios might occur. First, a narcissist might face a crisis in life that demonstrated the limitations of the egocentric orientation to life. Like people addicted to some drug, narcissists might deny their condition and need for a reorientation for a long time. When faced with a crisis, however, they might realize their narcissism cannot equip them for a meaningful life.

Second, a narcissist might become dissatisfied through a more gradual process of comparing his or her values with distinctively Christian values. Even though narcissism is common in our culture, some people resist the pull of culture and rise to the level of Christian values. Moses grew up feeling the pull of both Egyptian culture and Hebrew culture. The writer of Hebrews said that Moses identified with his fellow Hebrews even though he would suffer because he "had an eye for real values" (Heb. 11:26).[6] Sensing dissatisfaction with narcissism, a narcissist might begin to ask, why not the best?

If life experiences began to prompt such questions and comparison, a narcissist might feel two interrelated needs or hungers. First, a narcissist could develop a yearning for community. Narcissism can be lonely, and a narcissist might realize the truth of God's comment, "It is not good for the man to be alone" (Gen. 2:18a). In his search for a meaningful life, Koheleth realized that "Two are better than one" (Eccles. 4:9a, see 4:7-12).

Many television situation comedies highlight the value of family life as the group faces life's adversities and joys together. The theme song for the television series "Cheers" mentions how people love to congregate at a bar where everyone knows your name and is glad you came in to visit.

Second, a dissatisfied narcissist can also have a desire for a relationship with God. Once the common misconceptions of God as tyrant and ogre are cleared away, a narcissist might begin to realize that God is not a rival. Koheleth, for example, may be pointing to such a yearning for transcendence when he says, "He has also set eternity in the hearts of men" (Eccles. 3:11).

Robert Short began his study of movies about outer space by noting that humans have a "Christ-shaped vacuum" that can only be adequately filled by Christ.[7] Human restlessness is at root a search for God as well as a search for a meaningful life. A narcissist can find true fulfillment in life by finding a new vision of God and a relationship to him.

God's Calling Cards

If narcissists begin to experience a restlessness that cannot be quenched by their self-centeredness, they will find a God who has been reaching out to them. The human need is anticipated by a God who takes the initiative in meeting that need. A narcissist might ask, "But how will I know God is seeking me? I haven't seen God lately."

A common misconception is that God only appears in vivid and dramatic ways. Stories about Moses at the burning bush and Saul on the road to Damascus are often taken as the paradigms for divine revelation. Popular movies reinforce this limited understanding of God's self-disclosure. In *A Field of Dreams*, for example, a farmer hears a voice while working in his cornfield. Eventually he builds a baseball diamond in that field.

In the earlier *Oh, God* movies, God performs dramatic miracles to get people's attention. In the second movie, a young girl opens a fortune cookie and finds the message, "Meet me in the lounge. God." Puzzled, she opens another fortune cookie and reads, "I mean you, Tracy.—God." With these movie images in mind, many people besides narcissists mistakenly assume that God only speaks in the spectacular and unusual events of life.

Although God can reveal himself in these extraordinary ways, often God enters human life in more subtle ways. One famous preacher, for instance, discussed his call to the ministry by using the image of a tap on the shoulder.[8] A popular advertisement a few years ago insisted that you can get someone's attention with a whisper. Sometimes God whispers; sometimes God shouts. But God is always available to seekers. Evidence of God's existence and character might be compared to clues that point the seeker ultimately to God.

> Each of these clues has exactly the characteristics one would expect to find in the calling cards a God would leave of himself. They permeate human experience and are discernible by anyone, regardless of people's degree of education or sophistication. Nevertheless they are in no way coercive.[9]

The God of the Bible does not play the children's game of hide-and-seek with sincere seekers. Rather, God chooses to be available to all. "We search for the Searcher."[10]

God's availability to us is obvious in prayer. God invites us to pray, establishing a personal relationship that provides the meaning sought by narcissists and others. When the Hebrews felt God was not listening to them, Isaiah noted God's readiness to listen and respond to their prayers. "Before they call I will answer; while they are still speaking I will hear" (Isa. 65:24).

Two of Jesus' parables about prayer reinforce the availability of God in prayer. In the parable about the unexpected guest at night, Jesus urged his audience to ask, seek, and knock (Luke 11:5-10). If the sleepy neighbor will get out of bed to answer his door, surely God will respond to our prayers. In the parable about the persistent widow and the judge, Jesus emphasized that God would provide justice for his people (Luke 18:1-8).

Although God chooses to be revealed in a variety of ways, one constant source of a relationship with God is prayer. Prayer is not based on a narcissistic presumption that God is like a divine Santa Claus but on God's promise of willingness to hear and respond to our prayers. "It is God's promise that makes our prayer possible and that makes *the presumption which prayer is* possible for us."[11] God's calling cards may take a variety of forms, but prayer is a regular, consistent reminder of God's presence and responsiveness to humans.

Christ and Character

Christian prayer can transform character and make us more

Christlike. Narcissists are often motivated by a desire for a strong personal identity. They do not want to be just another face in the crowd. The experience of prayer can help them realize who they are and who they should be.

Narcissists may suffer from the delusion of self-sufficiency. They may believe they are really self-made people. Their reorientation to Christ rather than Narcissus can begin as they explore the question of self-identity more deeply.

While being interviewed on television about his autobiography, *Ragman's Son*, Kirk Douglas told of stopping to pick up a hitchhiker. When the man realized a famous actor was driving the car, he blurted out, "Do you know who you are?" Douglas commented that the question was a good one for all to confront. Prayer provides both the opportunity for a candid self-inventory and the starting point for real self-fulfillment.

The apostle Paul succinctly stated his own personal identity: "But by the grace of God I am what I am" (1 Cor. 15:10a). Grace does not eliminate all human effort and achievement in determining who we are. Rather, divine grace provides the ultimate foundation and context for personal identity. D. M. Baillie once referred to the relationship of divine grace and human responsibility as the paradox of grace.[12]

We can be proud of what we achieve in life without becoming narcissistic *if* our personal identity is rooted in the grace of God. Rather than debating who should get the credit for our achievements or our personal identity, we should acknowledge that ultimately we are who we are by the grace of God. Paul went on in the same passage to note that he worked hard. "No, I worked harder than all of them—yet not I, but the grace of God that was with me" (1 Cor. 15:10b). Awareness of divine grace does not lead to apathy or self-hate.

Through prayer we also become increasingly aware of God, and that relationship contributes to our identity as people of God. Recent studies on worship in general and prayer in particular have stressed that liturgy can affect our identity and our lifestyle. Although the primary purpose in worship is to focus attention on God, not ourselves, one by-product of the worship experience is a transformation of who we are.

> We do not worship God in order to become better people. Christians worship God simply because we are God's beloved ones. Christian worship is an intrinsic activity. But as we worship, something happens to us. The love we return in worship is, in turn, lovingly forming us for the better. The worship of the church . . . is a major context of moral formation.[13]

In worship and prayer we learn how to focus attention on God rather than ourselves. When we learn to "see" God more clearly, then we will see ourselves more clearly as well. *"A life formed by prayer is a life opposed to illusion, self-deception, and hypocrisy."*[14]

Prayer changes people. Any significant relationship has a transforming effect on character and identity. Psychologists note the influence of significant others on the formation of our personalities.[15] In prayer we encounter God, who becomes the supreme significant other in the shaping of our character.[16]

Prayer, by bringing us into intimate contact with God, has a transforming effect on the pray-er. Through a consistent pattern of encounters and dialogues with God, our deepest convictions, our character and identity, will become more Christlike.

Like most relationships with significant others, prayer will take time to transform us. A narcissist who prays will sense the tension between Christ and Narcissus. Christlikeness does not occur overnight. Because we "imitate whom we adore" we will increasingly show the character of the God to whom we pray.[17]

Once we encounter God in a meaningful way in conversion, the rest of life is a process of becoming Christlike. Through a lifetime of worship experiences we more and more identify with the God revealed in Jesus. A narcissist might profitably adopt the medieval prayer made famous in the play "Godspell":

> Day by day three things I pray,
> to see thee more clearly
> love thee more dearly
> follow thee more nearly.

Such a prayer reminds us that transformation takes time. "Day by day" praying provides us with the opportunity to be transformed, to become more Christ-centered and less self-centered.

Notes

Chapter 1

1 C. S. Lewis, *Letters to Malcolm: Chiefly on Prayer* (New York: Harcourt Brace Jovanovich, 1963), 82.

2. H. Richard Niebuhr, *Christ and Culture* (New York: Harper & Row, 1956, Torchbooks), 1-2. For a critique and updating of Niebuhr, see Charles Scriven, *The Transformation of Culture: Christian Social Ethics After H. Richard Niebuhr* (Scottdale, Pa.: Herald Press, 1988).

3 Ibid., 35-36.

4. Emil Brunner, *The Christian Doctrine of the Church, Faith, and the Consummation*, trans. David Cairns (Philadelphia: Westminster, 1962), 328.

5. "Pray-er" refers to the person praying and "prayer" refers to what the pray-er says.

6. Fisher Humphreys, *The Heart of Prayer* (Nashville: Broadman Press, 1980), 11. See also Theodore W. Jennings, Jr., *Life as Worship* (Grand Rapids: Eerdmans, 1982), 16-19; Donald G. Bloesch, *The Struggle of Prayer* (Colorado Springs: Helmers & Howard, 1988), 50-55.

7. C. K. Barrett, *The First Epistle to the Corinthians* (New York: Harper & Row, 1968), 144-153.

8. Jennings, 64.

9. Cf. David Miller, *The New Polytheism: Rebirth of Gods and Goddesses* (New York: Harper & Row, 1974).

10. For a brief discussion of "Some Defective Theories of Prayer," see George A. Buttrick, *Prayer* (Nashville: Abingdon, 1942), 47-59; see also, Stanley J. Grenz, *Prayer: The Cry for the Kingdom* (Peabody, Mass.: Hendrickson, 1988), 31-36.

11. Paul Tillich, *Dynamics of Faith* (New York: Harper & Row, 1957), 9-12.

12. For example, Eugene H. Peterson, *Earth & Altar: The Community of Prayer in a Self-Bound Society* (Downers Grove, Ill.: InterVarsity Press, 1985) proposes the

unselfing of America through a careful study of selected psalms. Robert H. Schuller, *Self-Esteem: The New Reformation* (Waco, Tex.: Word, 1982) examines the Lord's Prayer and distinguishes self-esteem from egotism.

Chapter 2

1. C. S. Lewis, *Mere Christianity* (New York: Macmillan, 1960), 171.

2. *Encyclopedia of Bioethics*, s.v. "Bioethics," by K. Danner Clouser.

3. Christopher Lasch, *The Culture of Narcissism: American Life in an Age of Diminishing Expectations* (New York: Warner Books, 1979), 29.

4. Aaron Stern, *Me: The Narcissistic American* (New York: Ballantine Books, 1979), 4-5.

5. Daniel Yankelovich, *New Rules: Searching for Self-Fulfillment in a World Turned Upside Down* (New York: Random House, 1981), 244-264.

6. Robert N. Bellah, et al., *Habits of the Heart: Individualism and Commitment in American Life* (Berkeley: University of California Press, 1985).

7. Robert E. Webber, *The Secular Saint: A Case for Evangelical Social Responsibility* (Grand Rapids: Zondervan, 1979). Webber developed these views in *The Church in the World: Opposition, Tension, or Transformation?* (Grand Rapids: Zondervan, 1986). The classic discussion is H. Richard Niebuhr, *Christ and Culture* (New York: Harper & Row, 1951).

8. Walter Brueggemann, *In Man We Trust: The Neglected Side of Biblical Faith* (Atlanta: John Knox Press, 1972), 13-14.

9. Paul Tillich, *Theology of Culture* (London: Oxford, 1959), 42.

10. John Wiley Nelson, *Your God Is Alive and Well and Appearing in Popular Culture* (Philadelphia: Westminster, 1976), 16. See also my essay, "Angels Unawares: Toward a Theology of Popular Culture," *Search* 17 (Fall 1986):7-12, and Andrew M. Greeley, *God in Popular Culture* (Chicago: Thomas More, 1988).

Chapter 3

1. For an extreme criticism of patriarchal language, see Mary Daly, *Beyond God the Father* (Boston: Beacon, 1973).

2. For a survey of two types of feminist theology, revolutionary and reformist, see Sallie McFague, *Metaphorical Theology* (Philadelphia: Fortress, 1982), 152-177.

3. For a scholarly study, see Hans Küng, *Does God Exist?* trans. Edward Quinn (Garden City, N.Y.: Doubleday, 1980); for a more popular defense of God's existence, see C. Stephen Evans, *The Quest for Faith* (Downers Grove, Ill.: InterVarsity, 1986).

4. John Wisdom's parable, quoted in John Hick, *Philosophy of Religion*, 2d ed. (Englewood Cliffs, N.J.: Prentice-Hall, 1973), 86.

5. Hick, 90-92.

6. *The Sunday Oklahoman*, December 15, 1985, Women's News 3.

7. Peter C. Hodgson, *Jesus-Word and Presence* (Philadelphia: Fortress, 1971), 2-3.

8. Richard Cunningham, *The Christian Faith and Its Contemporary Rivals* (Nashville: Broadman, 1988), 50-51.

9. Theodore W. Jennings, Jr., *Life as Worship* (Grand Rapids: Eerdmans, 1982), 18.

10. J. B. Phillips, *Your God Is Too Small* (New York: Macmillan, 1965).

11. For example, Andrew M. Greeley, *God in Popular Culture* (Chicago: Thomas More Press, 1988); Robert L. Short, *The Gospel According to Peanuts* (Richmond:

John Knox, 1964); and *The Gospel from Outer Space* (San Francisco: Harper & Row, 1983).

12. For a more philosophical treatment of rival views, see Norman Geisler, *Christian Apologetics* (Grand Rapids: Baker, 1976).

13. See Joseph B. Tyson, *The New Testament and Early Christianity* (New York: Macmillan, 1984), 125.

14. For a similar conclusion, see Douglas R. Groothuis, *Unmasking the New Age* (Downers Grove, Ill.: InterVarsity Press, 1986), 18-20.

15. For the relationship of the doctrine of God to prayer, see W. Bingham Hunter, *The God Who Hears* (Downers Grove, Ill.: InterVarsity, 1986); Donald G. Bloesch, *The Struggle of Prayer* (Colorado Springs: Helmers & Howard, 1988), 26-40; Don E. Saliers, "Prayer and the Doctrine of God in Contemporary Theology," *Interpretation* 34 (July 1980): 265-278.

16. Robert Farrar Capon, *The Third Peacock* (Garden City, N.Y.: Image, 1972), 59.

17. Millard J. Erickson, *Christian Theology* (Grand Rapids: Baker Book House, 1983), 1:263-300.

18. See Sallie McFague, *Models of God* (Philadelphia: Fortress, 1987), 33 for the is/is not distinction.

19. Joachim Jeremias, *The Central Message of the New Testament* (Philadelphia: Fortress, 1965), 19.

20. C. S. Lewis, *The Problem of Pain* (New York: Macmillan, 1962), 42-46.

21. For recent treatments of divine suffering, see Paul S. Fiddes, *The Creative Suffering of God* (Oxford: Clarendon Press, 1988) and my *The Passion of God* (Macon, Ga.: Mercer University Press, 1985).

22. Timothy F. Lull, "The Trinity in Recent Theological Literature," *Word & World* 2 (Winter 1982): 61.

23. Erickson, 1:342.

24. Shirley C. Guthrie, Jr., *Christian Doctrine* (Richmond: CLC Press, 1968), 89.

25. Joanne Marxhausen, *3 in 1* (St. Louis: Concordia, 1973).

26. For a recent adaptation, see Dale Moody, *The Word of Truth* (Grand Rapids: Eerdmans, 1981), 115-126.

Chapter 4

1. Richard J. Foster, *Money, Sex & Power* (San Francisco: Harper & Row, 1985), 187-188.

2. Arnold Lobel, *Frog and Toad Together* (New York: Harper & Row, 1971), 52–64.

3. Reinhold Niebuhr, *The Nature and Destiny of Man* (New York: Charles Scribner's Sons, 1941), l:178-207.

4. Henry Fairlie, *The Seven Deadly Sins Today* (Notre Dame: University of Notre Dame Press, 1979), 55.

5. On "Worm Theology," see Charles R. Swindoll, *Growing Strong in the Seasons of Life* (Portland: Multnomah Press, 1983), 247-248.

6. Guy Greenfield, *Self-Affirmation: The Life-Changing Force of a Christian Self-Image* (Grand Rapids: Baker, 1988), 118-121.

7. Douglas S. Looney, "Thank You, Pete Weber," *Sports Illustrated,* May 4, 1987, 27.

8. Fairlie, 40.

9. Henlee H. Barnette, *The Church and the Ecological Crisis* (Grand Rapids: Eerdmans, 1972).

10. Millard J. Erickson, *Christian Theology* (Grand Rapids: Baker, 1984), 2:615-618.

11. Jürgen Moltmann, *The Trinity and the Kingdom* (San Francisco: Harper & Row, 1981), 220, says: "Friendship with God finds its pre-eminent expression in prayer." For more development of God as Friend see Sallie McFague, *Models of God* (Philadelphia: Fortress, 1987), 157-180.

12. George A. Buttrick, *Prayer* (Nashville: Abingdon, 1942), 288.

13. Warren McWilliams, *Free in Christ* (Nashville: Broadman, 1984), 15-17.

14. Theodore Jennings, Jr., *Life as Worship* (Grand Rapids: Eerdmans, 1982), 99.

Chapter 5

1. For example, Donald B. Kraybill, *The Upside-Down Kingdom*, rev. ed., (Scottdale, Pa.: Herald Press, 1990), 20. For a readable overview of scholarly views on the kingdom, see Robert H. Stein, *The Method and Message of Jesus' Teachings* (Philadelphia: Westminster, 1978), 60-79.

2. William Dyrness, *Christian Apologetics in a World Community* (Downers Grove, Ill.: InterVarsity, 1983), 76.

3. Clarence Jordan, *The Cotton Patch Version of Matthew and John* (New York: Association, 1970), 28 (on Matt. 6:33). For a brief summary of Jordan's life, see James Wm. McClendon, Jr., *Biography as Theology* (Nashville: Abingdon, 1974), 112-139, and 126-127 on "movement" in Jordan's thought.

4. Wes Seeliger, *Western Theology* (Houston: Pioneer Ventures, 1973).

5. For example, William Barclay, *The Gospel of Matthew, Volume 1* (Philadelphia: Westminster, 1958), 210-213, argues for parallelism between kingdom of God and God's will being done. The danger of this view is the loss of the already/ not yet tension; the kingdom is not yet fully realized.

6. *New Yorker*, September 6, 1976.

7. Soren Kierkegaard, *Purity of Heart Is to Will One Thing* (New York: Harper & Row, 1948).

8. H. H. Rowley, *The Relevance of Apocalyptic* (New York: Association, 1963), 185, footnote, quoting J. K. Mozley.

9. H. Richard Niebuhr, *Christ and Culture* (New York: Harper & Row, 1956, Torchbooks), 5-7.

10. Donald G. Bloesch, *Essentials of Evangelical Theology* (San Francisco: Harper & Row, 1982), 1:28-29.

11. *USA Today*, April 4, 1986, 2D.

12. For discussions of *kenosis*, see Geddes MacGregor, *He Who Lets Us Be* (New York: Seabury, 1975), and Maggie Ross, *Pillars of Flame* (San Francisco: Harper & Row, 1988).

13. W. Bingham Hunter, *The God Who Hears* (Downers Grove, Ill.: InterVarsity, 1986), 57-58.

14. Harvey Cox, *The Secular City* (New York: Macmillan, 1966), 108.

15. For an evangelical response to liberation theologies, see Stanley Gundry and Alan Johnson, eds., *Tensions in Contemporary Theology*, exp. ed. (Chicago: Moody, 1979), 404-418.

16. E. Glenn Hinson, "Merton's Many Faces," *Religion in Life* 42 (Summer 1973):154. On the contemplative and active lives, see Donald G. Bloesch, *The Struggle of Prayer* (Colorado Springs: Helmers & Howard, 1988), 131-153.

Chapter 6
1. Marvin Hinten, *God Is Not a Vending Machine . . . So Why Do We Pray Like He Is?* (Grand Rapids: Zondervan, 1983).
2. George A. Buttrick, *Prayer* (Nashville: Abingdon, 1942), 79-82.
3. For an evangelical critique of Marx and Freud, see Anthony Campolo, *Partly Right* (Waco, Tex: Word, 1985), 104-193.
4. Anthony Campolo, Jr., *The Power Delusion* (Wheaton, Ill.: Victor, 1983), 117.
5. Donald E. Gowan, *The Triumph of Faith in Habakkuk* (Atlanta: John Knox, 1976), 9.
6. For a black perspective, see Ralph Ellison, *Invisible Man* (New York: Vintage Books, 1952), 3.
7. See Donald B. Kraybill, *The Upside-Down Kingdom*, rev. ed. (Scottdale, Pa.: Herald Press, 1990), 28-31, for a discussion of the relationship between spiritual and physical or social dimensions of the gospel.
8. Harold Kushner, *When All You've Ever Wanted Isn't Enough* (New York: Pocket Books, 1987), 62.
9. Bruce C. Birch and Larry L. Rasmussen, *Bible and Ethics in the Christian Life* (Minneapolis: Augsburg, 1976), 125-141.
10. Richard J. Foster, *Money, Sex & Power* (San Francisco: Harper & Row, 1985), 165-166.
11. C. S. Lewis, *The Magician's Nephew* (New York: Collier Books, 1955), 150.
12. Millard J. Erickson, *Christian Theology* (Grand Rapids: Baker Book House, 1983), 1:278-281.
13. C. S. Lewis, *Miracles* (New York: Macmillan, 1970), 180.
14. Fisher Humphreys, *The Heart of Prayer* (Nashville: Broadman, 1980), 55-59, uses the relation of a parent to a child to illustrate why some requests must be rejected.

Chapter 7
1. John Claypool, *Tracks of a Fellow Struggler* (Waco, Tex.: Word, 1974), 61-77.
2. A. M. Hunter, *A Pattern for Life*, rev. ed. (Philadelphia: Westminster, 1965), 74.
3. William Temple, *Nature, Man and God* (London: Macmillan, 1953), 478.
4. Clarence Jordan and Bill Lane Doulos, *Cotton Patch Parables of Liberation* (Scottdale, Pa.: Herald Press, 1976), 63.
5. Langdon Gilkey, *Shantung Compound* (New York: Harper & Row, 1975), 111.
6. Richard J. Foster, *Celebration of Discipline* (San Francisco: Harper & Row, 1978), 69-83, and *Freedom of Simplicity* (San Francisco: Harper & Row, 1981).
7. Ronald J. Sider, *Rich Christians in an Age of Hunger* (Downers Grove, Ill.: InterVarsity, 1977).
8. Clarence Jordan, *The Cotton Patch Version of Matthew and John* (New York: Association Press, 1970), 20.
9. Anthony Campolo, *A Reasonable Faith* (Waco, Tex.: Word, 1983), 117-118.
10. Millard J. Erickson, *Christian Theology* (Grand Rapids: Baker, 1984), 2:539, uses this term at the end of his defense of conditional unity as the Christian view of human nature.

Chapter 8
1. Bruce M. Metzger, *The New Testament: Its Background, Growth, and Content* (Nashville: Abingdon, 1965), 221.

2. Wayne Oates, *Confessions of a Workaholic* (Waco, Tex.: Word, 1972).

3. For a classic study of Christology and soteriology, see D. M. Baillie, *God Was in Christ* (New York: Charles Scribner's Sons, 1948).

4. Jaroslav Pelikan, *Jesus Through the Centuries* (New Haven: Yale University Press, 1985) provides a fascinating study of images of Jesus.

5. Ernst Kasemann, *Jesus Means Freedom* (Philadelphia: Fortress, 1972). Pelikan, 206-219, argues that Jesus as liberator is the dominant image in the nineteenth and twentieth centuries. See also my *Free in Christ* (Nashville: Broadman, 1984) for a fuller treatment of the New Testament view of freedom.

6. For a brief discussion of *hilasterion*, see Donald Guthrie, *New Testament Theology* (Downers Grove, Ill.: InterVarsity, 1981), 468-469.

7. C. S. Lewis, *The Lion, the Witch and the Wardrobe* (New York: Collier, 1970). For a defense of the ransom theory, see Charles Taliaferro, "A Narnian Theory of the Atonement," *Scottish Journal of Theology* 41 (1988):75-92.

8. C. S. Lewis, *God in the Dock* (Grand Rapids: Eerdmans, 1970), 181.

9. For balanced studies of the major atonement theories, see Fisher Humphreys, *The Death of Christ* (Nashville: Broadman, 1978), and Paul S. Fiddes, *Past Event and Present Salvation: The Christian Idea of the Atonement* (Louisville: Westminster, 1989).

10. C. S. Lewis, *The Screwtape Letters* (New York: Macmillan, 1978), 36-37.

11. Martin Marty, *A Cry of Absence* (San Francisco: Harper & Row, 1983).

12. Theodore W. Jennings, Jr., *Life as Worship* (Grand Rapids: Eerdmans, 1982), 104.

13. F. F. Bruce, *Philippians* (San Francisco: Harper & Row, 1983), 125.

14. M. Scott Peck, *The Road Less Travelled* (New York: Simon and Schuster, 1978), 19.

Chapter 9

1. Karl Menninger, *Whatever Became of Sin?* (New York: Hawthorn Books, 1973).

2. "Sin," *People*, February 10, 1986, 107-109.

3. Reinhold Niebuhr, *The Nature and Destiny of Man* (New York: Charles Scribner's Sons, 1964), 1:222.

4. *Shawnee News-Star*, December 1, 1967, 6.

5. T. B. Maston, *Biblical Ethics* (Waco, Tex.: Word, 1967), 167-168, highlights Jesus' stress on the internal.

6. H. Richard Niebuhr, *Christ and Culture* (New York: Harper & Row, Torchbooks, 1956), 187.

7. Reinhold Niebuhr, 228-240; S. Dennis Ford, *Sins of Omission* (Minneapolis: Fortress, 1990).

8. Erich Fromm, *Escape from Freedom* (New York: Avon, 1941).

9. Harvey Cox, *On Not Leaving It to the Snake* (New York: Macmillan, 1967), xiv.

10. Peter C. Hodgson, *New Birth of Freedom* (Philadelphia: Fortress, 1976), 173-206, presents a liberation theology perspective on personal and collective expressions of sin.

11. Terence E. Fretheim, *The Suffering of God* (Philadelphia: Fortress, 1984), 107-127, discusses God's suffering due to a broken relationship.

12. William L. Blevins, "The Early Church: Acts 1-5," *Review and Expositor* 71 (Fall 1974): 473.

13. Lewis Smedes, *Forgive and Forget* (San Francisco: Harper & Row, 1984), 24-25.

14. Corrie Ten Boom and Jamie Buckingham, *Tramp for the Lord* (Old Tappan, N.J.: Fleming H. Revell, 1974), 55-57.

Chapter 10
1. Theodore W. Jennings, Jr., *The Liturgy of Liberation: The Confession and Forgiveness of Sins* (Nashville: Abingdon, 1988) is a helpful discussion of confession in public worship.

2. Clarence Jordan and Bill Lane Doulos, *Cotton Patch Parables of Liberation* (Scottdale, Pa.: Herald Press, 1976), 38-42.

3. Thomas Harris, *I'm OK, You're OK* (New York: Harper & Row, 1969).

4. William Barclay, *The Mind of St. Paul* (New York: Harper & Row, 1958), 202-203.

5. Paul Tillich, *The Shaking of the Foundations* (New York: Charles Scribner's Sons, 1948), 161-162.

6. Frank Stagg, *New Testament Theology* (Nashville: Broadman, 1962), 137-138.

7. C. S. Lewis, *The Great Divorce* (New York: Macmillan, 1946), 72.

Chapter 11
1. C. S. Lewis, *The Screwtape Letters* (New York: Macmillan, 1978), 3.

2. Frank E. Peretti, *This Present Darkness* (Westchester, Ill.: Crossway, 1986).

3. Peter C. Hodgson, *New Birth of Freedom* (Philadelphia: Fortress, 1976), 195-206.

4. For example, Richard J. Foster, *Money, Sex & Power* (San Francisco: Harper & Row, 1985), 180-183, 186-189; Walter Wink, *Naming the Powers* (Philadelphia: Fortress, 1984), 104-113. For various interpretations of Satan and demonic powers, see John P. Newport, *Life's Ultimate Questions* (Dallas: Word, 1989), 185-216.

5. C. S. Lewis, *The Lion, the Witch and the Wardrobe* (New York: Collier, 1970), 29-39.

6. James Taylor, *A Porcine History of Philosophy and Religion* (Nashville: Abingdon, 1972).

7. Dorothee Soelle, *Suffering* (Philadelphia: Fortress, 1975), 73.

8. For a review of several biblical perspectives on suffering, see Newport, 229-235.

9. Shirley C. Guthrie, Jr., *Christian Doctrine* (Richmond: CLC Press, 1968), 171.

10. Frances Havergal, "Like a River Glorious," *Baptist Hymnal* (Nashville: Convention Press, 1975), no. 208, v. 3.

11. Daniel J. Simundson, *Faith Under Fire* (Minneapolis: Augsburg, 1980), 17-41.

12. G. Leibholz, "Memoir," in Dietrich Bonhoeffer, *The Cost of Discipleship*, rev. ed. (New York: Macmillan, 1963), 28.

13. For a fuller statement on the biblical views of suffering, see my *When You Walk Through the Fire* (Nashville: Broadman, 1986).

14. Robert Browning Hamilton, "Along the Road," in John Bartlett, *Familiar Quotations*, 11th ed. (Boston: Little, Brown, and Co., 1941), 861.

15. C. S. Lewis, *The Problem of Pain* (New York: Macmillan, 1962), 93.

16. James H. Cone, *God of the Oppressed* (New York: Seabury, 1975), 183-194.

17. John Paterson, *The Book That Is Alive* (New York: Charles Scribner's Sons, 1954), 90-91.

Chapter 12
1. Peter C. Hodgson, *New Birth of Freedom* (Philadelphia: Westminster, 1976), 61-63.

2. For a general discussion of laments, see Bernhard W. Anderson, *Out of the Depths*, rev. and expand. ed. (Philadelphia: Westminster, 1983), 63-105.

3. For an older treatment, see Gerhard von Rad, "The Confessions of Jeremiah," in *Theodicy in the Old Testament*, ed. James L. Crenshaw (Philadelphia: Fortress, 1983), 88-99.

4. C. S. Lewis, *Reflections on the Psalms* (New York: Harcourt, Brace, Jovanovich, 1958), 12.

5. For a review of several responses to the absence of God, see David O. Woodyard, *The Opaqueness of God* (Philadelphia: Westminster, 1970).

6. Daniel J. Simundson, *Faith Under Fire* (Minneapolis: Augsburg, 1980), 44.

7. M. Scott Peck, *The Road Less Traveled* (New York: Simon and Schuster, 1978), 15.

8. Garrison Keillor, *Leaving Home* (New York: Viking, 1987), xv.

9. Theodore W. Jennings, Jr., *The Liturgy of Liberation* (Nashville: Abingdon, 1988), 112-114. See also, Guthrie, 183-184. Jürgen Moltmann, *Theology of Hope*, trans. James W. Leitch (London: SCM, 1967), 24-26, uses Prometheus and Sisyphus to illustrate two forms of hopelessness, presumption, and despair.

10. Theodore W. Jennings, Jr., *Life as Worship* (Grand Rapids: Eerdmans, 1982), 30.

11. Oscar Cullmann, *Christ and Time*, trans. by Floyd V. Filson (London: SCM Press, 1951), 84-88; Robert H. Stein, *The Method and Message of Jesus' Teachings* (Philadelphia: Westminster, 1978), 77.

12. See a fuller statement in John Newport, *What Is Christian Doctrine?* (Nashville: Broadman, 1984), 34-42.

13. For the origin of this prayer, see Bob E. Patterson, *Reinhold Niebuhr* (Waco, Tex.: Word, 1977), 19-20.

Chapter 13
1. Richard J. Foster, *Money, Sex & Power* (San Francisco: Harper & Row, 1985), 180. Thomas C. Oden, *Agenda for Theology* (San Francisco: Harper & Row, 1979, 37-41, identifies "narcissistic hedonism" as one of the major features of the late twentieth century.

2. William H. Willimon, *The Service of God: How Worship and Ethics Are Related* (Nashville: Abingdon, 1983), 11.

3. Cited in John R. W. Stott, "Am I Supposed to Love Myself or Hate Myself?" *Christianity Today*, April 20, 1984, 26.

4. Theodore W. Jennings, Jr., *Life as Worship* (Grand Rapids: Eerdmans, 1982), 99.

5. Fyodor Dostoevski, *The Brothers Karamazov*, trans. by David Magarshack (New York: Penguin, 1958), 299.

6. Adapted from Paul Tillich, *Systematic Theology* (Chicago: University of Chicago, 1951), 1:147-150.

7. John B. Cobb, Jr., and David Ray Griffin, *Process Theology* (Philadelphia: Westminster, 1976), 52-57.

8. Anthony Campolo, *A Reasonable Faith* (Waco, Tex.: Word, 1983), 162-178.

9. Gene Outka, *Agape: An Ethical Analysis* (New Haven: Yale University Press, 1972), 55-74. See also Henlee H. Barnette, *Introducing Christian Ethics* (Nashville: Broadman, 1961), 101-110; Norman L. Geisler, *Ethics: Alternatives and*

Issues, (Grand Rapids: Zondervan, 1971), 139-157; Paul Brownback, *The Danger of Self-Love* (Chicago: Moody Press, 1982); Guy Greenfield, *Self-Affirmation: The Life-Changing Force of a Christian Self-Image* (Grand Rapids: Baker, 1988), 147-159.

10. Geisler, 152.

11. Lewis Smedes, *Mere Morality* (Grand Rapids: 1983), 160-161.

12. C. S. Lewis, *The Great Divorce* (New York: Macmillan, 1946).

13. Arthur C. McGill, *Suffering: A Test of Theological Method* (Phildelphia: Westminster, 1982), 57.

14. Bernard of Clairvaux, *Treatises II: The Steps of Humility and Pride; On Loving God* (Kalamazoo, Mich.: Cistercian Publications, 1980), 115-121. For a brief commentary, see E. Glenn Hinson, *Seekers After Mature Faith* (Waco, Tex.: Word, 1968), 71-72.

15. Geroge R. Lucan, Jr., and Thomas W. Ogletree, *Lifeboat Ethics* (New York: Harper & Row, 1976).

16. Adapted from my essay, "Christian Ministers as Problem-Solvers," *Search* 20 (Summer, 1990): 22-26.

17. M. Scott Peck, *The Road Less Traveled* (New York: Simon and Schuster, 1978), 15.

18. Lewis B. Smedes, *Choices: Making Right Decisions in a Complex World* (San Francisco: Harper & Row, 1986), chapter 6.

19. Cited in Margaret Miles, *Fullness of Life* (Philadelphia: Westminster, 1981), 9.

20. Joseph Campbell with Bill Moyers, *The Power of Myth* (New York: Doubleday, 1988), 5.

21. Jennings, 10.

22. Geoffrey Wainwright, *Doxology: The Praise of God in Worship, Doctrine, and Life* (New York: Oxford University Press, 1980), 218.

23. Willimon, 73-74.

Chapter 14

1. John Paterson, *The Book That Is Alive: Studies in Old Testament Life and Thought as Set Forth by the Hebrew Sages* (New York: Charles Scribner's Sons, 1974), 140.

2. Ibid.

3. Harold Kushner, *When All You've Ever Wanted Isn't Enough* (New York: Pocket Books, 1987), 179.

4. Paterson, 150. See also Wayne H. Peterson, "Ecclesiastes," *The Broadman Bible Commentary,* ed. Clifton J. Allen (Nashville: Broadman, 1971), 5:106.

5. Augustine, *The Confessions of St. Augustine,* trans. Rex Warner (New York: New American Library, 1963), 17.

6. Clarence Jordan, *The Cotton Patch Version of Hebrews and the General Epistles* (New York: Association, 1973), 37.

7. Robert L. Short, *The Gospel from Outer Space* (San Francisco: Harper & Row, 1983), 15.

8. Peter Marshall, *Mr. Jones, Meet the Master,* ed. Catherine Marshall (New York: Pyramid Books, 1966), 19-29.

9. C. Stephen Evans, *The Quest for Faith: Reason and Mystery as Pointers to God* (Downers Grove, Ill.: InterVarsity, 1986), 49. For more on "clues" to God's reality, see Evans, 31-60.

10. T. B. Maston, *Why Live the Christian Life?* (Nashville: Broadman, 1974), 3. See Evans, 61-67, on "The Divine Suitor."

11. Theodore W. Jennings, Jr., *Life as Worship* (Grand Rapids: Eerdmans, 1982), 32.

12. D. M. Baillie, *God Was in Christ* (New York: Charles Scribner's Sons, 1948), 114-118.

13. William H. Willimon, *The Service of God: How Worship and Ethics Are Related* (Nashville: Abingdon, 1983), 37. For "Liturgical Contributions to Christian Character Formation," see 48-72. For "Prayer as Formation" and "Praise as Formation," see Jennings, 62-80, 110-124.

14. Jennings, 67 (emphasis in original). See Willimon, 67-68.

15. Anthony Campolo, *A Reasonable Faith* (Waco, Tex.: Word, 1983), 158-162.

16. Guy Greenfield, *Self-Affirmation: The Life-Changing Force of a Christian Self-Image* (Grand Rapids: Baker, 1988), 21.

17. Willimon, 90.

Bibliography

"Ann Landers." *The Sunday Oklahoman*, December 15, 1985, Women's News 3.

"Sin." *People*, February 10, 1986, 107-109.

Anderson, Bernhard W. *Out of the Depths*. Rev. and exp. ed. Philadelphia: Westminster, 1983.

Augustine. *The Confessions of St. Augustine*. Translated by Rex Warner. New York: New American Library, 1963.

Baillie, D. M. *God Was in Christ*. New York: Charles Scribner's Sons, 1948.

Barclay, William. *The Gospel of Matthew, Volume 1*. Philadelphia: Westminster, 1958.

_____. *The Mind of St. Paul*. New York: Harper & Row, 1958.

Barnette, Henlee H. *The Church and the Ecological Crisis*. Grand Rapids: Eerdmans, 1972.

_____. *Introducing Christian Ethics*. Nashville: Broadman, 1961.

Barrett, C. K. *The First Epistle to the Corinthians*. New York: Harper & Row, 1968.

Bellah, Robert N. et al. *Habits of the Heart: Individualism and Commitment in American Life*. Berkeley: Unversity of California Press, 1985.

Bernard of Clairvaux. *Treatises II: The Steps of Humility and Pride: On Loving God*. Kalamazoo, Mich.: Cistercian Publications, 1980.

Birch, Bruce C. and Larry L. Rasmussen. *Bible and Ethics in the Christian Life*. Minneapolis: Augsburg, 1976.

Blevins, William L. "The Early Church: Acts 1-5." *Review and Expositor* 71 (Fall 1974): 463-474.

Bloesch, Donald G. *The Struggle of Prayer.* Colorado Springs: Helmers & Howard, 1988.

_____. *Essentials of Evangelical Theology.* 2 vols. San Francisco: Harper & Row, 1982.

Bonhoeffer, Dietrich. *The Cost of Discipleship.* Rev. ed. New York: Macmillan, 1963.

Brownback, Paul. *The Danger of Self-love.* Chicago: Moody Press, 1982.

Bruce, F. F. *Philippians.* San Francisco: Harper & Row, 1983.

Brueggemann, Walter. *In Man We Trust: The Neglected Side of Biblical Faith.* Atlanta: John Knox Press, 1972.

Brunner, Emil. *The Christian Doctrine of the Church, Faith, and the Consummation.* Translated by David Cairns. Philadelphia: Westminster, 1962.

Buttrick, George A. *Prayer.* Nashville: Abingdon, 1942.

Campbell, Joseph and Bill Moyers. *The Power of Myth.* New York: Doubleday, 1988.

Campolo, Anthony, Jr. *The Power Delusion.* Wheaton, Ill.: Victor, 1983.

_____. *Partly Right.* Waco, Tex.: Word, 1985.

_____. *A Reasonable Faith.* Waco, Tex.: Word, 1983.

Capon, Robert Farrar. *The Third Peacock.* Garden City, N.Y.: Image, 1972.

Claypool, John. *Tracks of a Fellow Struggler.* Waco, Tex.: Word, 1974.

Cobb, John B., Jr., and David Ray Griffin. *Process Theology.* Philadelphia: Westminster, 1976.

Cone, James H. *God of the Oppressed.* New York: Seabury, 1975.

Cox, Harvey. *The Secular City.* New York: Macmillan, 1966.

_____. *On Not Leaving It to the Snake.* New York: Macmillan, 1967.

Cullmann, Oscar. *Christ and Time.* Translated by Floyd V. Filson. London: SCM Press, 1951.

Cunningham, Richard. *The Christian Faith and Its Contemporary Rivals.* Nashville: Broadman, 1988.

Daly, Mary. *Beyond God the Father.* Boston: Beacon, 1973.

Dostoevski, Fyodor. *The Brothers Karamazov.* Translated by David Magarshack. New York: Penguin, 1958.

Dyrness, William. *Christian Apologetics in a World Community.* Downers Grove, Ill.: InterVarsity, 1983.

Ellison, Ralph. *Invisible Man.* New York: Vintage Books, 1952.

Encyclopedia of Bioethics. S.v. "Bioethics," by K. Danner Clouser.

Erickson, Millard J. *Christian Theology.* Vol. 1. Grand Rapids: Baker Book House, 1983.

Erickson, Millard J. *Christian Theology.* Vol. 2. Grand Rapids: Baker Book House, 1984.

Evans, C. Stephen. *The Quest for Faith.* Downers Grove, Ill.: InterVarsity, 1986.

Fairlie, Henry. *The Seven Deadly Sins Today*. Notre Dame: University of Notre Dame Press, 1979.

Fiddes, Paul S. *The Creative Suffering of God*. Oxford: Clarendon Press, 1988.

_____. *Past Event and Present Salvation: The Christian Idea of the Atonement*. Louisville: Westminster, 1989.

Ford, S. Dennis. *Sins of Omission*. Minneapolis: Fortress, 1990.

Foster, Richard J. *Money, Sex & Power*. San Francisco: Harper & Row, 1985.

_____. *Celebration of Discipline*. San Francisco: Harper & Row, 1978.

_____. *Freedom of Simplicity*. San Francisco: Harper & Row, 1981.

Fretheim, Terence E. *The Suffering of God*. Philadelphia: Fortress, 1984.

Fromm, Erich. *Escape from Freedom*. New York: Avon, 1941.

Geisler, Norman L. *Ethics: Alternatives and Issues*. Grand Rapids: Zondervan, 1971.

_____. *Christian Apologetics*. Grand Rapids: Baker, 1976.

Gilkey, Langdon. *Shantung Compound*. New York: Harper & Row, 1975.

Gowan, Donald E. *The Triumph of Faith in Habakkuk*. Atlanta: John Knox, 1976.

Greenfield, Guy. *Self-Affirmation: The Life-Changing Force of a Christian Self-Image*. Grand Rapids: Baker, 1988.

Greeley, Andrew M. *God in Popular Culture*. Chicago: Thomas More, 1988.

Grenz, Stanley J. *Prayer: The Cry for the Kingdom*. Peabody, Mass.: Hendrickson, 1988.

Groothuis, Douglas R. *Unmasking the New Age*. Downers Grove, Ill.: InterVarsity, 1986.

Gundry, Stanley and Alan Johnson, eds. *Tensions in Contemporary Theology*. Exp. ed. Chicago: Moody, 1979.

Guthrie, Donald. *New Testament Theology*. Downers Grove, Ill.: InterVarsity, 1981.

Guthrie, Shirley C., Jr. *Christian Doctrine*. Richmond: CLC Press, 1968.

Harris, Thomas. *I'm OK, You're OK*. New York: Harper & Row, 1969.

Havergal, Frances. "Like a River Glorious." *Baptist Hymnal*. Nashville: Convention Press, 1975.

Hick, John. *Philosophy of Religion*. 2d ed. Englewood Cliffs, N.J.: Prentice-Hall, 1973.

Hinson, E. Glenn. "Merton's Many Faces." *Religion in Life* 42 (Summer 1973): 153-167.

_____. *Seekers After Mature Faith*. Waco, Tex.: Word, 1968.

Hinten, Marvin. *God Is Not a Vending Machine . . . So Why Do We Pray Like He Is?* Grand Rapids: Zondervan, 1983.

Hodgson, Peter C. *Jesus-Word and Presence*. Philadelphia: Fortress, 1971.

_____. *New Birth of Freedom*. Philadelphia: Fortress, 1976.

Humphreys, Fisher. *The Heart of Prayer*. Nashville: Broadman Press, 1980.

Hunter, A. M. *A Pattern for Life*. Rev. ed. Philadelphia: Westminster, 1965.

Hunter, W. Bingham. *The God Who Hears*. Downers Grove, Ill.: Inter-Varsity, 1986.

Jennings, Theodore W., Jr. *Life as Worship*. Grand Rapids: Eerdmans, 1982.

_____. *The Liturgy of Liberation: The Confession and Forgiveness of Sins*. Nashville: Abingdon, 1988.

Jeremias, Joachim. *The Central Message of the New Testament*. Philadelphia: Fortress, 1965.

Jordan, Clarence. *The Cotton Patch Version of Matthew and John*. New York: Association, 1970.

_____. *The Cotton Patch Version of Hebrews and the General Epistles*. New York: Association, 1973.

Jordan, Clarence and Bill Lane Doulos. *Cotton Patch Parables of Liberation*. Scottdale, Pa.: Herald Press, 1976.

Kasemann, Ernst. *Jesus Means Freedom*. Philadelphia: Fortress, 1972.

Keillor, Garrison. *Leaving Home*. New York: Viking, 1987.

Kierkegaard, Soren. *Purity of Heart Is to Will One Thing*. New York: Harper & Row, 1948.

Kraybill, Donald B. *The Upside-Down Kingdom*. Scottdale, Pa.: Herald Press, 1978. Rev. ed. 1990.

Küng, Hans. *Does God Exist?* Translated by Edward Quinn. Garden City, N.Y.: Doubleday, 1980.

Kushner, Harold. *When All You've Ever Wanted Isn't Enough*. New York: Pocket Books, 1987.

Lasch, Christopher. *The Culture of Narcissism: American Life in an Age of Diminishing Expectations*. New York: Warner Books, 1979.

Lewis, C. S. *Letters to Malcolm: Chiefly on Prayer*. New York: Harcourt Brace Jovanovich, 1963.

_____. *God in the Dock*. Grand Rapids: Eerdmans, 1970.

_____. *The Great Divorce*. New York: Macmillan, 1946.

_____. *The Lion, the Witch and the Wardrobe*. New York: Collier, 1970.

_____. *The Magician's Nephew*. New York: Collier Books, 1955.

_____. *Mere Christianity*. New York: Macmillan, 1960.

_____. *Miracles*. New York: Macmillan, 1970.

_____. *The Problem of Pain*. New York: Macmillan, 1962.

_____. *Reflections on the Psalms*. New York: Harcourt, Brace, Jovanovich, 1958.

_____. *The Screwtape Letters*. New York: Macmillan, 1978.

Lobel, Arnold. *Frog and Toad Together*. New York: Harper & Row, 1971.

Looney, Douglas S. "Thank You, Pete Weber." *Sports Illustrated*, May 4, 1987, 27.

Lucan, George R., Jr., and Thomas W. Ogletree. *Lifeboat Ethics*. New York: Harper & Row, 1976.

Lull, Timothy. "The Trinity in Recent Theological Literature." *Word & World* 2 (Winter 1982): 61-68.

MacGregor, Geddes. *He Who Lets Us Be*. New York: Seabury, 1975.

Marshall, Peter. *Mr. Jones, Meet the Master*. Ed. Catherine Marshall. New York: Pyramid Books, 1966.

Marty, Martin. *A Cry of Absence*. San Francisco: Harper & Row, 1983.

Marxhausen, Joanne. *3 in 1*. St. Louis: Concordia, 1973.

Maston, T. B. *Biblical Ethics*. Waco, Tex.: Word, 1967.

_____. *Why Live the Christian Life?* Nashville: Broadman, 1974.

McClendon, James Wm., Jr. *Biography as Theology*. Nashville: Abingdon, 1974.

McFague, Sallie. *Metaphorical Theology*. Philadelphia: Fortress, 1982.

_____. *Models of God*. Philadelphia: Fortress, 1987.

McGill, Arthur C. *Suffering: A Test of Theological Method*. Philadelphia: Westminster, 1982.

McWilliams, Warren. "Angels Unawares: Toward a Theology of Popular Culture." *Search* 17 (Fall 1986): 7-12.

_____. "Christ or Narcissus? Ministry in a Self-Centered Culture." *Search* 19 (Fall 1988): 14-20.

_____. "Christian Ministers as Problem-Solvers." *Search* 20 (Summer 1990): 22-26.

_____. *Free in Christ*. Nashville: Broadman, 1984.

_____. *The Passion of God*. Macon, Ga.: Mercer University Press, 1985.

_____. *When You Walk Through the Fire*. Nashville: Broadman, 1986.

Menninger, Karl. *Whatever Became of Sin?* New York: Hawthorn Books, 1973.

Metzger, Bruce M. *The New Testament: Its Background, Growth, and Content*. Nashville: Abingdon, 1965.

Miles, Margaret. *Fullness of Life*. Philadelphia: Westminster, 1981.

Miller, David. *The New Polytheism: Rebirth of Gods and Goddesses*. New York: Harper & Row, 1974.

Moltmann, Jürgen. *The Trinity and the Kingdom*. Translated by Margaret Kohl. San Francisco: Harper & Row, 1981.

_____. *Theology of Hope*. Translated by James W. Leitch. London: SCM, 1967.

Moody, Dale. *The Word of Truth*. Grand Rapids: Eerdmans, 1981.

Nelson, John Wiley. *Your God Is Alive and Well and Appearing in Popular Culture*. Philadelphia: Westminster, 1976.

New Yorker, September 6, 1976.

Newport, John P. *Life's Ultimate Questions*. Dallas: Word, 1989.

—————————. *What Is Christian Doctrine?* Nashville: Broadman, 1984.

Niebuhr, H. Richard. *Christ and Culture*. New York: Harper & Row, Torchbooks, 1956.

Niebuhr, Reinhold. *The Nature and Destiny of Man*. New York: Charles Scribner's Sons, 1941.

Oates, Wayne. *Confessions of a Workaholic*. Waco, Tex.: Word, 1972.

Oden, Thomas C. *Agenda for Theology*. San Francisco: Harper & Row, 1979.

Outka, Gene. *Agape: An Ethical Analysis*. New Haven: Yale University Press, 1972.

Paterson, John. *The Book That Is Alive*. New York: Charles Scribner's Sons, 1954

Patterson, Bob E. *Reinhold Niebuhr*. Waco, Tex.: Word, 1977.

Peck, M. Scott. *The Road Less Traveled*. New York: Simon and Schuster, 1978.

Pelikan, Jaroslav. *Jesus Through the Centuries*. New Haven: Yale University Press, 1985.

Peretti, Frank E. *This Present Darkness*. Westchester, Ill.: Crossway, 1986.

Peterson, Eugene H. *Earth & Altar: The Community of Prayer in a Self-Bound Society*. Downers Grove, Ill.: InterVarsity Press, 1985.

Peterson, Wayne H. "Ecclesiastes." In *The Broadman Bible Commentary*. Ed. Clifton J. Allen. Nashville: Broadman, 1971.

Phillips, J. B. *Your God Is Too Small*. New York: Macmillan, 1965.

Ross, Maggie. *Pillars of Flame*. San Francisco: Harper & Row, 1988.

Rowley, H. H. *The Relevance of Apocalyptic*. New York: Association, 1963.

Saliers, Don E. "Prayer and the Doctrine of God in Contemporary Theology." *Interpretation* 34 (July 1980): 265-278.

Schuller, Robert H. *Self-Esteem: The New Reformation*. Waco, Tex.: Word, 1982.

Scriven, Charles. *The Transformation of Culture: Christian Social Ethics After H. Richard Niebuhr*. Scottdale, Pa.: Herald Press, 1988.

Seeliger, Wes. *Western Theology*. Houston: Pioneer Ventures, 1973.

Shawnee News-Star, December 1, 1967, 6.

Short, Robert L. *The Gospel According to Peanuts*. Richmond: John Knox, 1964.

—————————. *The Gospel from Outer Space*. San Francisco: Harper & Row, 1983.

Sider, Ronald J. *Rich Christians in an Age of Hunger*. Downers Grove, Ill.: InterVarsity, 1977.

Simundson, Daniel J. *Faith Under Fire*. Minneapolis: Augsburg, 1980.

Smedes, Lewis B. *Choices: Making Right Decisions in a Complex World*. San Francisco: Harper & Row, 1984.

—————————. *Forgive and Forget*. San Francisco: Harper & Row, 1984.

_____. *Mere Morality*. Grand Rapids: Eerdmans, 1983.

Soelle, Dorothee. *Suffering*. Philadelphia: Fortress, 1975.

Stagg, Frank. *New Testament Theology*. Nashville: Broadman, 1962.

Stein, Robert H. *The Method and Message of Jesus' Teachings*. Philadelphia: Westminster, 1978.

Stern, Aaron. *Me: The Narcissistic American*. New York: Ballantine Books, 1979.

Stott, John R. W. "Am I Supposed to Love Myself or Hate Myself?" *Christianity Today*, April 20, 1984, 26-28.

Swindoll, Charles R. *Growing Strong in the Seasons of Life*. Portland: Multnomah Press, 1983.

Taliaferro, Charles. "A Narnian Theory of the Atonement." *Scottish Journal of Theology* 41 (1988): 75-92.

Taylor, James. *A Porcine History of Philosophy and Religion*. Nashville: Abingdon, 1972.

Temple, William. *Nature, Man and God*. London: Macmillan, 1953.

Ten Boom, Corrie and Jamie Buckingham. *Tramp for the Lord*. Old Tappan, N.J.: Fleming H. Revell, 1974.

Tillich, Paul. *Dynamics of Faith*. New York: Harper & Row, 1957.

_____. *The Shaking of the Foundations*. New York: Charles Scribner's Sons, 1948.

_____. *Systematic Theology*. Vol. 1. Chicago: University of Chicago, 1951.

_____. *Theology of Culture*. London: Oxford, 1959.

Tyson, Joseph B. *The New Testament and Early Christianity*. New York: Macmillan, 1984.

USA Today, April 4, 1986, 2D.

von Rad, Gerhard. "The Confessions of Jeremiah." In *Theodicy in the Old Testament*. Edited by James L. Crenshaw. Philadelphia: Fortress, 1983.

Wainwright, Geoffrey. *Doxology: The Praise of God in Worship, Doctrine, and Life*. New York: Oxford University Press, 1980.

Webber, Robert E. *The Secular Saint: A Case for Evangelical Social Responsibility*. Grand Rapids: Zondervan, 1979.

_____. *The Church in the World: Opposition, Tension, or Transformation?* Grand Rapids: Zondervan, 1986.

Willimon, William H. *The Service of God: How Worship and Ethics Are Related*. Nashville: Abingdon, 1983.

Wink, Walter. *Naming the Powers*. Philadelphia: Fortress, 1984.

Woodyard, David D. *The Opaqueness of God*. Philadelphia: Westminster, 1970.

Yankelovich, Daniel. *New Rules: Searching for Self-Fulfillment in a World Turned Upside Down*. New York: Random House, 1981.

The Author

Warren McWilliams teaches at Oklahoma Baptist University, occupying the Auguie Henry Chair of Bible. He is a graduate of Oklahoma Baptist University (B.A.), The Southern Baptist Theological Seminary (M.Div.), and Vanderbilt University (M.A., Ph.D.). He specializes in theology and ethics. Previously he taught at Stetson University in Deland, Florida.

McWilliams has written three other books, *Free in Christ: The New Testament Understanding of Freedom* (Broadman, 1984), *The Passion of God: Divine Suffering in Contemporary Protestant Theology* (Mercer University Press, 1985), and *When You Walk Through the Fire* (Broadman, 1986). He has written numerous articles and book reviews and is a frequent contributor of curriculum materials for his denomination. He also wrote for the *Disciple's Study Bible* and the *Mercer Dictionary of the Bible.*

A native of Fort Smith, Arkansas, McWilliams lives in Shawnee, Oklahoma, with his wife, Patty, and his daughters Amy and Karen. He is active in the University Baptist Church and frequently preaches and teaches in Oklahoma churches.